BEYOND THE HERE AND NOW

BEYOND THE HERE AND NOW

JEFF ASTLEY & DAVID DAY

CARTOONS BY NOEL FORD

A LION BOOK

Copyright © 1996 Jeff Astley and David Day

The authors assert the moral right
to be identified as the authors of this work

Published by
Lion Publishing plc
Sandy Lane West, Oxford, England
ISBN 0 7459 2365 8
Albatross Books Pty Ltd
PO Box 320, Sutherland, NSW 2232, Australia
ISBN 0 7324 1469 5

First edition 1996
10 9 8 7 6 5 4 3 2 1 0

A catalogue record for this book is available
from the British Library

Printed and bound in Great Britain
by Cox & Wyman Ltd, Reading

Thanks

We enjoyed writing this book. This does not mean that it was not hard work, only that it was very enjoyable hard work.

Of course we had help. Most of those who helped did so unknowingly, by encouraging and provoking us to see beyond our everyday concerns and to find meaning in the whole of life. Inevitably our wives and children (and, where appropriate, their wives and children) provoked us most. But colleagues and friends helped in that way too. Thank you all.

A particular word of thanks should go to Dorothy Greenwell who patiently typed and re-typed the text, and positively refused to complain even when we started all over again (twice). Thanks too should go to the North of England Institute for Christian Education, especially for the coffee.

Jeff Astley
David Day

Durham
January 1996

Contents

Of Teaspoons, Keyholes and Sausages...

It doesn't matter how carefully you check the washing-up bowl; there will be a teaspoon left in the bottom when you empty the water. Just when you think you have stuck the paper to the wall it detaches itself and floats gracefully towards the floor. The milk in the pan refuses to come to the boil until you go to answer the doorbell. As you step back to admire the car you have just cleaned a bird leaves its own little contribution on the bonnet. *Typical!*

The golden rule of archaeology is that if you dig here the treasure will be over there. On the other hand if you dig over there it will be here... The French have a saying, 'When the house is full, granny gives birth to twins.' The humorist Paul Jennings elevated all this to a philosophy which he called resistentialism. Its motto is, 'Things are against us.' And its fundamental principle can be demonstrated by dropping a large number of slices of buttered toast at random. A significant majority will land on the carpet buttered side down. It's the teaspoon in the bottom of the washing-up bowl again.

Starting here?
There's the beginning of a world view here. And it goes something like this: 'Everything in the universe is constantly ganging up on us. Typical experiences suggest a world which is malevolently determined to make sure we get our come-uppance.'

This may, of course, be just an infantile reaction. And we may just be paranoid. Still, as Douglas Adams has pointed out, it's odd that ticket machines in car-parks are always 18.4 cm away from your outstretched fingertips, however long your arms. Do they adjust themselves as you drive up? Hmmm...

This book is based on the assumption that from time to time we all catch ourselves reflecting on such quirks and glitches. We are such creatures as muse, ponder, cogitate and mull over. We note, mark and pore. At a pinch we may even ruminate.

And almost any situation can make us do it. There seems to be no limit to the experience which can call forth the reaction, 'That's odd', 'I wonder why...', 'Why is it that...?' Sometimes we're more ambitious and not content with saying 'Coo' or 'Well, there's a thing!', we leap into metaphysical mode. 'That's typical!', 'There's something in people which always...', 'Life's like that.'

Is it sensible to do this? To let one small part of the universe stand for or point towards the whole? Is there any good reason why a teaspoon should represent the essence of Life? Not when you put it that way. But it is extremely odd that we don't seem able to kick the habit. In this kind of situation we may often suspect that we are reading meaning *into* what we experience. Is it equally possible that we could be reading meaning *out* of things, that in some way it was embedded in the event? Is the universe like a string of sausages where you get hold of one end and are led inevitably to the other? There doesn't seem to be an easy answer.

But we all have moments of vision which seem to be windows into some larger reality. Such peepholes give us a keyhole-sized view of what lies on the other side of the door.

They may be rather special experiences—on mountains, by waterfalls, in thunderstorms. They may be personally unsettling—a narrow escape, a bitter loss, the birth of a child. They may be utterly ordinary and mundane—trusting a friend, having an argument, washing up, the smell of wood smoke.

Peter Berger, an eminent sociologist, has argued that some of our most ordinary actions can become signals of another kind of reality. 'Signals of transcendence', he calls them. A mother comforting a baby, people at play, gestures of courage in the face of death—these are all essentially human forms of behaviour.

But Berger asks if they also point beyond themselves to something fundamentally true about ourselves and the way the world is made. Are they signals of order, eternity or ultimate justice which may be found in a reality somewhere *beyond* the one we immediately experience? Do the ordinary experiences of life come to us 'freighted' with cargo from another reality if we will only take the time to unload it? Is the world, both the world we observe and the inner world of our feelings and experiences, there to be 'read'? Or is it completely opaque and unintelligible?

What is certain is that we are congenitally incapable of *not* finding meaning in things. A kiss can't be reduced to a bare description of 'osculatory behaviour'. A sophisticated set of codes tells us whether this particular kiss is a perfunctory peck, an absent-minded greeting, a guilty act of trying to make up for forgetting an anniversary, an expression of affection or the begin-ning of an erotic encounter. We'll make some sense of it, one way or another.

We have already hinted that seeing what is very specific as an illustration of a larger reality takes us into the whole business of world views. 'Sod's Law' is a comment about the universe and the way it runs. When we go *'beyond* the here and now' we start to make claims about Everything That Exists.

In the same way each section of this book starts with what is local, specific, personal, under your nose, common-or-garden human experience and pushes it to see what it might mean in terms of God, Life, the Universe and Everything. That's the method.

And ending where?

Our end point is not entirely a surprise. Since the authors of this book are both Christians, we believe that the Christian world-view is the most comprehensive and illuminating explanation of human experience. Like any world-view it has something to say about absolutely everything, from why gloss paint glosses to life after death. This may be somewhat irritating to those who prefer a small-scale approach, but that's world-views for you. They are like picture frames. Everything is included in the picture. Nothing falls outside the frame. If it did, you wouldn't have a proper *world* view. So we can't really apologize for the all-inclusive nature of

Christianity. However, we hope it's possible to hold all-inclusive views in an amiable and good-tempered way.

There's one more feature of the book which we'd like to point out before you start. We've thought it worthwhile not just to express the Christian vision of the world but also to include a little of the debate about that vision which has gone on within the church. For two thousand years Christians have argued about the best way to state their vision adequately, accurately, consistently, systematically and comprehensively without falling into nonsense while still remaining true to the original experience. Sometimes the discussion has floated off into the lunacy of arguing about how many angels can stand on a pinhead. (Mind you, even that is not without interest.) Generally Christian theology represents an extraordinarily persistent and impressive attempt to think clearly. We think that many people will be glad to eavesdrop on that discussion.

All this makes the book more of an invitation than a tract or a lecture. It starts from shared human experience. It commends a particular interpretation. It shows how that interpretation connects with other beliefs and values to form an overall vision. But in this, it's like trying to get a friend to appreciate your favourite piece of music or see why you rave over a painting.

Trispen: a form of intelligent grass. It grows a single tough stalk and makes its home on lawns. When it sees the lawnmower coming it lies down and pops up again after it has gone by.
Goole: The puddle on the bar into which the barman puts your change.

Douglas Adams and John Lloyd

From the whirling womb of time come millions of men and their feet crowd the earth and they cut one another's throats for room to stand and among them all are not two thumbs alike. Somewhere is a great God of Thumbs who can tell the inside story of this.

Carl Sandberg

14

From World to God?

If God had anything to do with making the world, it seems a safe bet that looking at the world will give us some idea of what God is like. People's cars, houses, children reflect their personalities, so we can play a similar game on a larger scale. It's worth a try, anyway...

1 God is Green...

A Precious World?

No one who has looked a cat straight in the eye can ever seriously believe that human beings are a superior form of creation. No animal comes and goes with such freedom as a cat. No animal is capable of such withering glances as a cat. Cats are cool and laid back. Within three weeks of its arrival any decent cat has trained its 'owner' (a misnomer if ever there was one) to do its absolute bidding.

The idea of a superior order of creation is a peculiarly human invention. Is the liver fluke inferior to the sheep, within whose body it finds nourishment? Are fleas among the lower orders, the proles and plebs of the environment? There are food chains, it's true, but often it's difficult to see who will come out on top in the end, as the ghoulish song 'On Ilkley Moor baht 'at'

suggests. In fact, maybe it's easier to see what's going on as a gigantic co-operative, with worker and management roles totally confused.

Human beings tend to draw the line at this. Look in the cat's eyes and you'll see nothing answering you. The stare you get in return is blank, uncomprehending and alien. Therefore the world out there is inferior, to be mastered and dominated. Most living things are our enemies, fit only to be swatted, sprayed, shot, snared or flushed down the plughole. Wolves are our natural enemies. The giant octopus is greatly to be feared, the 'devilfish' of the oceans.

Just occasionally we get a different message. A nature programme on television demonstrates that according to all the evidence wolves are really rather decent to one another, unlikely to attack humans without good cause and the victims of a couple of thousand years of media misrepresentation. Not long ago the BBC programme 'Wildlife on One' showed amazing footage of underwater camerawoman Victoria Stone having her face 'explored' by a giant 'devilfish'. As the probing tentacles accidentally dislodged the air supply from her mouth Ms Stone gently replaced it and allowed the octopus to continue its patient investigation. The episode was reminiscent of two friends getting to know each other.

The global hooligan?

But where has the idea that humanity is a superior species, at enmity with the rest of creation, come from? Scientist Lynn White once laid the blame firmly at the door of Christianity. He argued that we have an ecological crisis precisely because the original mandate to Adam and Eve gave them the right to 'subdue the earth' and have 'dominion over the fish of the sea and the birds of the air'. No wonder humanity is at odds with nature. As a result of this doctrine of dominion, we have felt free to abuse the environment, treating it as an inexhaustible supply of goods designed solely for our satisfaction. There will not be an earth to enjoy if we continue to burn up the rainforests, destroy the ozone layer, accelerate global warming, consume fossil fuels, dump toxic waste, annihilate endangered species, produce acid rain and pump 20 million cubic metres of sewage every day into the North Sea. (It has been said that swimming in the sea has given new meaning to the phrase 'going through the motions'.) The process of turning the world from supermarket to rubbish dump owes a lot to the Christian doctrine of humanity's right to be ruthless towards creation.

Properly understood, however, the biblical witness suggests something quite different. The earth is a gift from the hand of the Creator and is therefore of incalculable worth. This encourages the notion that the created world has 'rights'. Everything comes from the hand of God. Everything belongs ultimately to him.

There have always been those capable of raising this sense of oneness with the created world to the level of a vision. Francis of Assisi, for example, seems to have had the knack. He spoke of 'Brother Sun' and 'Sister Moon', and called fish and birds his brothers and sisters. There are dozens of odd tales about Francis and the animal kingdom. But the most moving illustration of his sense of unity with creation comes from an incident at the end of his life when he was seriously ill. His physicians decided that his ear would have to be cauterized with a red-hot iron. Francis spoke to the fire, 'Brother Fire, deal gently with me for the love I have always had for you in the Lord.'

It may be a matter of seeing the environment as 'creation', itself issuing from the hand of God. It may be the sense that the earth has 'rights' or is in some way 'a gift' to be used responsibly. It may result from the realization that living things can feel pain in much the same way as ourselves. All such understandings can result in a 'mystical' or almost 'religious' view of the world.

Does matter matter?

If the world is a gift then matter has status. There have been versions of Christianity which have despised the earthy, considering it evil and looking forward to a moment when the spiritual essence of humanity could be released from its prison.

But if the earth is a gift then matter is not something inferior and unfortunately mucky. At its best Christianity rejoices in the earthy, or at least that is what we claim in Chapter 35. Human beings should not aspire to be angels as if flesh were a rather unfortunate goof on the part of the Almighty. The authentic biblical voice is echoed in the Jewish prayer for going to the loo: 'Blessed art thou, O Lord our God, King of the Universe, who hast made me a creature of pipes and openings...'

If the world is really God's world we have a responsibility to handle it thankfully. It is here that we find the heart of the Christian environmental ethic. This entails using it according to its nature, neither abusing nor destroying nor polluting it but sharing it, profiting from it and delighting in it. Does it much matter if a species ceases to exist? That the dodo is as dead as a dodo? That pandas, red kites and orchids are threatened with extinction? According to this view, to accelerate the destruction of a species is a sort of blasphemy. This vision of the universe is one of abundance, variety and complexity. Like a divine Mozart, God continues to spin symphonies, sonatas, quartets and concertos of living things out of his head. 'The valleys stand so thick with corn that even they are singing.' He, whose being has no end, 'fathers them forth'. To which the only proper response is *Amen*—'let it be so'.

And on any reckoning, a cormorant covered in crude oil, its wings flapping impotently, comes very close to blasphemy.

When I carefully consider the curious habits of dogs
I am compelled to conclude
that man is the superior animal.
When I consider the curious habits of man
I confess, my friend, I am puzzled.

Ezra Pound

---

2 And Every Bush Afire...

An Awesome World?

'It's getting nearer. For God's sake let's get indoors!'

The violent energy of a thunderstorm or hurricane both fascinates us and fills us with dread. The rarer natural wonders of earthquakes and volcanic eruptions do the same. This is nature rising up to destroy. Terrified though we are, we cannot turn our eyes from it.

'I am become the Destroyer of Worlds,' whispered the physicist Robert Oppenheimer on witnessing the detonation of the first atomic bomb, quoting the words of the 'All-Highest' from a Hindu holy book. Yet one storm cloud can easily contain more energy than that explosion. A single streak of lightning may be charged with 100 million volts of power. Within a millionth of a second it can create a temperature of 30,000°C/50,000°F—five

times the temperature at the surface of the sun.

Contemplating other wonders of nature can be less frightening, but equally fascinating and breathtaking: the complex inner workings of the atom, the microscopic architecture of a tiny organism, the majesty of one of the great mammals or extinct reptiles. How intricate, how beautiful and how awe-inspiring nature can be. Above all, perhaps, we wonder at the vastness of the unconquerable sea. To be out on the deep over 70,000 fathoms of water is an awesome thing. It is not surprising that it is an experience that has been used as an image of faith (see Chapter 21).

Wondering at the world is natural. Isaac Newton, the founder of classical physics, spoke of his achievements as those of a child sitting on the beach surrounded by a vast stretch of pebbles, shells, rocks and sand, examining playfully just a handful of what was all around him. Scientists are fascinated by nature, fascinated enough to try to understand it. But what we understand is a tiny part of what there is to understand. On our planet alone most of the sea remains unexplored; and although about a million species of insects have been named, this certainly represents only a fraction of those yet unrecorded. Even our scientific understanding of everyday, accessible things is continually being deepened, revised and transcended.

From nature to supernature

The wonders of nature, spectacular or everyday, may offer us a window onto religious faith. The experience of awe, dread and fascination that can come over us as we pause breathless on a mountaintop, or peer down a microscope, is close to the experience that some have called 'the experience of the holy'. They say that God, the Divine Being who is beyond nature, is *supernatural*.

God is other than and different from the things in the universe. But a *taste* of what it might be like to experience such a being comes from the heart-stopping, addictive experience of wondering at the world.

The idea of the holy

The holiness of God is mainly a matter of God's being set apart from all created things. God is 'wholly other': daunting, mysterious, terrifying. Rudolf Otto's book *The Idea of the Holy* coined the phrase 'numinous experience' to describe the encounter of created human beings with this inexpressible and majestic Creator.

Holiness has often been felt as an almost physical quality, like radioactivity: to be approached with caution and only after proper insulation. So in the Old Testament the high priest was the only person who was able to enter the Holy of Holies in the innermost reaches of the temple without risk of death, just as the holy mountain of Sinai where God gave Moses the Ten Commandments once had to be fenced off from the people of Israel. In the presence of a holy God the whole earth 'should keep silence'. Awe, dread and worship are the only proper responses. Holiness here is much more than moral goodness, it is something unique and distinctly religious.

But the numinous experience of awe (dread, terror, godly fear) is tempered with fascination. God is experienced as the daunting *but entrancing* 'wholly other'. God is dreadful; but those who meet God cannot tear themselves away. Otto writes of 'the hushed, trembling, and speechless humility of the creature in the presence of—whom or what? In the presence of that which is a *Mystery* inexpressible and above all creatures.'

He recognized that there are everyday, *finite* tastes of this experience, including those occasions when we 'shudder' at the thought of the unknown in the dark forest or under the sofa. The film *Close Encounters of the Third Kind* offered a bigger version of the same thing. In the final reel the scientists set up a rendezvous with the aliens and various small, but perfectly formed, UFOs buzz past to enthusiastic applause. But one techie, poring over his dials, notes that they show no signs of biological life. And then...

Then over the mountaintop comes something bigger and more spectacular than anything any of them could have conceived. The observers fall silent. In the cinema too the audience's reaction is close to the dread and fascination of the numinous. We are filled with awe.

Yet that Daddy-of-All-UFOs is presumably as a child's toy compared with the awe-inspiring, shudder-evoking grandeur of the presence of God.

The awe-ful God of the Bible

At the end of the Book of Job, after Job has argued with, questioned and challenged God, the holy God reveals himself in his power and mystery 'out of the whirlwind'. Here is the God who created the stars and the hippopotamus, lightning and wild horses. Job is overcome by this numinous experience:

> *Job answered the Lord:*
> *I know that you can do all things*
> *and that no purpose is beyond you...*
> *I knew of you then only by report,*
> *but now I see you with my own eyes.*
> *Therefore I yield,*
> *repenting in dust and ashes.*
> JOB 42:2, 5–6 (REB)

Other biblical texts present similar experiences: Moses before the burning bush in which he discerned God's presence; the prophet Isaiah's vision of God's glory in the temple; the disciples suddenly recognizing the awesomeness of Jesus' person and purpose on the Mount of Transfiguration, and the fearful mystery of his resurrection. The awesomeness of God is particularly well expressed in another passage from the Old Testament:

> *What likeness, then, will you find for God*
> *or what form to resemble his?...*
> *God sits enthroned on the vaulted roof of the world,*
> *and its inhabitants appear as grasshoppers.*
> *He stretches out the skies like a curtain,*
> *spreads them out like a tent to live in;*

He reduces the great to naught
and makes earthly rulers as nothing...
Do you not know, have you not heard?
The LORD, the eternal God,
creator of earth's farthest bounds,
does not weary or grow faint;
his understanding cannot be fathomed.

ISAIAH 40:18, 22–23, 28 (REB)

This is the holiness that takes your breath away...

Earth's crammed with heaven,
And every common bush afire with God;
And only he who sees takes off his shoes;
The rest sit round it and pluck blackberries.

Elizabeth Barrett Browning

3 That's About the Size of It...

A God-Sized World?

In the sixteenth century, human beings were put in their place by the dawning recognition that we were not, after all, the centre of the universe. The earth was a planet going round the sun. As astronomy advanced and the size of the cosmos became clearer, our place at the edge of a vast galaxy, itself but one of a myriad of star clusters, robbed us of our cosy sense of security and significance. Modern knowledge of the universe can make it seem an even more unnerving place.

❑ Ancient
The universe is perhaps about 13,500 million years old. We aren't.

Imagine that the universe were one year old. Then the oldest human being now alive would have been born one fifth of a second ago; whereas life would have begun on earth over fifteen weeks ago. This brings our lifespan into perspective. But it also underlines the vast age of the cosmos.

❑ Huge
Its immense size also beggars imagination. Astronomers measure it in 'light years' and 'light hours'. Our galaxy of stars is 100,000 light years wide. The nearest star to our own sun is 4.5 light years away. Our solar system itself is eleven light hours wide. A light year is the distance light can travel in one year, travelling at 299,728 kilometres per second (186,282 miles per second). So one light year is 9,411,109,000,000 kilometres or 5,874,600,000,000 miles

(and one light hour is 1,079,028,000 kilometres or 670,620,000 miles). That's big.

The universe itself is bigger. The observable universe, when viewed from earth, is at least 25 thousand million light years in diameter. That makes it over 240 thousand million million million (240,000,000,000,000,000,000,000,000) kilometres wide—ignoring the mileage! And that is only what we can observe by light and radio emissions. So the universe is bigger even than that. To make things worse it is continually expanding. It's hard to keep up.

❏ Dead?

There are at least 100,000 million galaxies in the known universe. Our galaxy, the Milky Way, itself contains over 100,000 million stars. One of them is our sun, with its system of nine planets. Many other stars must have their own planets. Some of them must be similar to our earth, with conditions suitable for the existence of the sort of life forms that we know. But most of it is either empty or lifeless—empty space, dead planets and their moons, or lifeless balls of stupifying, fiery heat.

The universe is vast. We lose count as we contemplate it. It is not surprising that as people look up at the sky on a starry night some are gripped, not by awe at the wonder of God, but by a deep sense of the cold, empty, impersonal *loneliness* of space. Can there be a caring God who made all of this?

The eternal silence of these infinite spaces frightens me.

Blaise Pascal

Is God too small?

Before human beings ever knew the vast age and size of the universe they felt a similar awe beneath the night sky that seemed to dwarf them:

> *When I look up at your heavens,*
> *the work of your fingers,*
> *at the moon and the stars*
> *you have set in place,*
> *What is a frail mortal,... a human being,*
> *that you should take notice of him?*
> PSALM 8:3–4 (REB)

For many, a vast, impersonal universe was and is a great denial of the existence of a personal, caring God. The cosy God at the end of our personal telephone line becomes increasingly implausible in a universe that big. Is the Christian idea of God too small to cope with all this?

A range of responses have been offered to this challenge...

Size isn't everything

Perhaps we should not be overimpressed by size and numbers. Herbert Samuel called that attitude 'a kind of cosmic snobbery'. Small can be beautiful too, and significant. Human beings are smaller than dinosaurs, but does than mean they are less important? Mozart died at the age of thirty-five, yet he created more than most people who live to be ninety.

Just because the universe is enormous, it need not dwarf our sense of our significance. After all, size isn't everything.

God beyond?

A more extreme response to the 'problem of size' would be to treat the idea of a personal God as totally inadequate picture language, only suitable for a childish religion. The true God, some say, is completely different from that—more like an impersonal force than a Heavenly Father.

This is the idea of *God beyond God*, similar to the notion in some Eastern religions of some 'Absolute' or impersonal reality behind the universe.

Creator

Or we may just admit that our cosy, domestic image of God must go. God may be the one who 'counts all the hairs' on our heads, and who knows 'when a single sparrow falls'; but this caring, involved God also 'made these stars' and 'drills them like an army'. The God of the Old Testament was recognized as the Creator of the whole universe, the God of the cosmos. And such a God must surely be big enough—and complex enough—to oversee the vast, complex order of creation. A caring, intimate God can still manage to cope with all of this.

On this more orthodox view God is *personal*, but not a limited *person* like us. Christians call God 'father', meaning that he cares and acts like a parent—creating, providing, loving. But he is not literally a father figure, or a 'big Daddy-in-the-Sky'. A God who creates a universe like ours cannot be simpler to understand than the universe he creates. Modern science, particularly the 'new physics', shows us a very complex and puzzling world. A domestic, carpet-slippered, rather dozy God could not have created it. A more grown-up concept of God is needed: an idea of one who is God enough for this God-sized task.

The majesty of space, and the graciousness of One who cares even for the little human beings who are lost within it, can both be seen as signs of the majesty of God.

4 Out of Control...

A Providential World?

Horoscopes are very popular. Many newspapers and magazines run them regularly. Some radio and TV channels do the same. Why? Because *we* read them. We listen to them.

Some people take horoscopes very seriously, seeking individual predictions based on the precise time of their date of birth. Most are content with the blanket coverage of the mass horoscope. Surveys show that not many of us are willing to say we 'believe in' them. But we still read them.

Q: DO YOU BELIEVE IN...? (FROM MORI, 1989)

God	76%
The Devil	37%
Astrology	37%
	(44% of women, 30% of men)
Opinion Polls	56%

THE FUTURE, FATE, LUCK ETC (FROM LEEDS SURVEY, 1982)

The number of people who think these things are important in making them what they are:

Fate and destiny	28%
Luck	30%
God	47%
My choices and decisions	74%

Are there times when you think the events of your life are predetermined by some higher force?

Yes	50%*
No	44%

*But 40% think we can't know even part of this plan

'It's just a bit of fun.' That's our half-embarrassed excuse. But why is it? And is it more than that?

Horoscopes or the horrors?

In the weeks before getting the results of an examination or a medical diagnosis, or in the hours before reading a casualty list of the train crash, pit disaster or battle, people often say that the waiting is almost worse than the bad news. 'It's not knowing that is the terrible thing.'

The horror of the future is partly a horror of the unknown. If only we *knew* what was going to happen, what was coming next, we should be forewarned and forearmed. We would feel more 'in control'—even if there is nothing we could possibly do about the future. (Except, perhaps, to stay in bed all day.)

Is that why we try to learn about our future, even through horoscopes? Knowing the future, or playing at knowing the future, takes away the horror of the unknown.

Knowledge and power

Knowledge, they say, is power. And if we had knowledge of the future—of which horse will win the 2.30, which shares will rise on the stock market or what numbers will come up in the National Lottery—we should have power. Foreknowledge would help us provide better for ourselves and our children. We would be less 'improvident' in our actions if we knew where they were leading. This is the sort of control we sometimes desperately desire over our lives and our destinies.

What do we mean?

Perhaps our desire for horoscopes is also a craving for meaning. If we could see the next page of the story it would feel more like a *story*. Instead of being just one accidental event after another, our lives might have a plot. They might seem to be going somewhere. And if my life is affected by Jupiter and the constellations, well, this great universe must be part of my story and I must be a part of its story.

Science tells me that I am a part of the world. Religion tells me I have a right to be here. And the horoscope is perhaps just a version of the same message:

'You have significance. You are part of a cosmic story.'

But is the price of this significance too high a price to pay? The horoscope suggests a closed future, and an impersonal law of fate. We might prefer an open future, and a caring cosmos. We might prefer reality to say, 'I love you. Fear not. All shall be well.' But failing that we yearn to hear it say, at least, 'I note your existence. Fear a little. Oh... and tomorrow you will be unlucky in love.'

Just a bit of fun?
If we sneak another look at today's horoscope, 'just for a bit of fun', maybe we're just playing a game with ourselves. It's the game of possibilities. 'What if I were to meet that tall dark stranger?' 'What if I were to stand up to people more?' The cold predictions of a closed future, in which Mars determines my fate, is not really what I want. I do, however, want to play the 'what if...' game. What if my life were different? But if I am free, and if the universe allows me freedom, and our future is 'not in our stars but in ourselves', then things *could* be different. Would that be 'fun' any more? Or would it be more a matter of facing the horror of the unknown with a new courage: the courage that, whatever the future throws at us, we can cope?

Providence
Religious people sometimes speak of God's 'providence'. The word literally means 'seeing before' or 'seeing on behalf of'. God, they claim, sees what is to happen next. He just knows. And he prepares for the future: he sees about it, he *provides* for his children. This far-seeing care is a mark of God, as it is the mark of a good parent. 'Being provided for' is at the heart of our sense of security, which gives us freedom to be ourselves. And like a good parent, God will not cushion us from the pain of reality but give us the courage to deal with it.

But God's providence is his foreknowledge, not ours. We do not know the future, Christians say, but we know that God knows it. Whatever shall be, shall be: not because it is controlled by stars and an ultimate, impersonal law of cause and effect, but because it is in God's hands. Our future is God's future. We don't know *what* will happen, but God can be trusted. The unknown future can be faced in trust and hope.

So there are at least two views of the universe open to us:

❑ EITHER our life and future is controlled by the stars, and we have no say in it. In the end, whatever will be, will be. It has all been fixed, unalterable for eternity. This is a possible view; but remember that the stars won't care, because they are just stars.

❑ OR we have some, though limited, control over our lives. Therefore we have a bit of a say in what comes next. Whatever will be will be, but now that is partly as a result of our decisions. And on this view, we may claim, at least the God of the universe will care, one way or the other, what we choose and what happens.

Is predestination predestined?

Predestination is the belief that God does not just know the future, in particular about who will be saved. He has also decided it or 'foreordained' it. In the fourth century St Augustine argued that God chooses ('elects') from eternity those who will have faith and those who will not. How else, he argued, can God's will be supreme? But the followers of the British monk Pelagius disagreed, claiming that humans have a God-given freedom that enables them to resist God's grace for them, so that human salvation is partly a matter of human choice and responsibility.

Centuries later John Calvin argued most forcefully a doctrine of 'double predestination' of some to heaven and others to hell, through God's sheer will. But his contemporary Arminius—who influenced John Wesley and Methodism—rejected this view, arguing that though God's grace is absolutely essential for faith, yet it can be resisted by free human beings.

Even within Christianity, then, there are different ways of thinking of the future, and of our role in it.

5 More Than Meets the Eye...

A Spiritual World?

If you are into alternative medicine then you really are spoilt for choice nowadays. It's no longer a matter of old-style acupuncture and operations without anaesthetic. Now you can try aromatherapy, ayurvedic medicine, chiro-practic, colour therapy, gem essence therapy, homeopathy, hypnosis, mud therapy, rogerian therapy, moxibustion, thalassotherapy and Zen or transcendental meditation. And the Prince of Wales has made it terribly respectable or at least, only slightly offbeat. Even talking to flowers may be worth a try—if all else fails. It can't do any harm.

Since the sixties something of a quiet revolution has been sweeping over Britain. The musical *Hair* brought the idea of the Age of Aquarius into the language of popular culture. As we near the end of the millennium the Earth will move backwards in the zodiac. Then the age of Pisces, which began about the time of the birth of Christ, will come to an end and a New Age, that of Aquarius, will begin. The growth of alternative medicine is just one marker signalling this revolutionary change of consciousness.

It is, of course, very easy to mock the New Age mentality. 'I'm sorry, officer, I was following my third eye' might not get you off a speeding charge. And Jehovah's Witnesses on the doorstep might back away if you said, 'Not today, thank you, we're Druids.' But the New Age seems to be here to stay.

Many of its basic techniques are beginning to be used even in the hard-headed world of business and manage-ment training. Medicine has had to take account of a less mechanistic view of the body. New Age concern to live in harmony with nature has led to a less exploitative attitude to the environment. New Age bookshops will cover topics from Tarot cards to non-competitive games; from reincarnation to total massage; from dowsing to natural childbirth. Is it possible that New Age ideas are pointing us to something important which we might have forgotten in a headlong rush for a fast buck, a quick lay and a cheap thrill?

Cheesed off with nothing-buttery?

The New Age belongs to the spirit. It is all too easy to seek a materialistic explanation for everything. A mysterious experience, a strange encounter is 'nothing but... what you had for supper last night... your hormones playing you up again... a trick of the light'. Seen with the inner eye the world of the senses is interpenetrated with another world, that of the spirit. 'The New Age movement' has become an umbrella term for a variety of philosophies, religions and quasi-religions which emphasize that there is more to reality than meets the eye. In fact, those who can see nothing more than what is staring them in the face are afflicted with a form of spiritual myopia. New Agers are impatient with people who deny the possibility of seeing with the inner eye, who are unenlightened and think that the world of the senses is all that there is.

> If you don't see me as God, it's because you don't see yourself as God.
>
> Shirley MacLaine

Release the genius within you!

Deep down within each one of us lies the real person, a self which can operate at a higher level of fulfilment than we would ever believe possible. The key to super-living is to tap the hidden, psychic resources that lie dormant and unused for most people, most of the time. We can each be transformed. This belief has given rise to a new gnosticism or cult of secret knowledge. Possession of the secret knowledge can unlock my potential. Often there are techniques to be learned or a discipline to be undertaken. And very often there are gurus or learned masters from whom alone the mystic wisdom can be obtained. New Age has brought to prominence a host of 'psychotechnologies'—chanting, biofeedback, transcendental meditation, Silva mind control, rebirthing, channelling, Est, Synanon. At the heart of many of these techniques lies the ability to visualize the unseen. By creating a new kind of reality in the mind, by the power of the imagination, an individual's personality can be changed. Creative capacities can be released, failure can become success, self-esteem enhanced, assertiveness increased. In some cases it is believed that visualizations can affect the chemistry of the body; cancerous cells can be destroyed and replaced with healthy ones.

Flying on an astral plane

From such a viewpoint it is not surprising to find that individuals claim to be able to travel to an alternate reality, an astral plane, projecting their consciousness into a totally different world. The anthropologist Carlos Castaneda is said to have made a number of such journeys 'through the crack between the worlds', with the aid of mind-altering substances. Shamans are equally capable of stepping into other realities. Even the role-playing game Dungeons and Dragons transports the players into a universe where time is different, which is subject to spiritual laws and where mysterious powers may be called upon. Astrology becomes a science which can tap into the planetary forces which undergird and dominate this world. Eastern religions which stress the impermanent or illusory nature of matter can show that New Age ideas are very ancient indeed.

Acupuncture and reflexology assume the need to match Yin and Yang energies in the body and presuppose that the body is an elaborate network of routes along which the life force or Qi travels. Aurasomatherapy uses herbal extracts and oils in a system of colour therapy which will revitalize the human aura, that invisible envelope of energy which surrounds all human beings.

Where does your lap go when you stand up?

Why is a mouse like when it spins?

May the force be with you!
In the opinion of many New Agers modern medicine has lost touch with nature. As it has become more and more scientific and technical it has increasingly seen the body as a defective machine, an engine to be tinkered with rather than a person to be healed. The New Age approach stresses holistic medicine. It is important to realize, however, that the whole is not just the individual—body, mind, spirit and emotions—but includes the individual in relationship with the rest of nature. Alternative medicine becomes particularly important in cases of illness without a known cure.

Typically, New Age medicine will stress that a person is more than just a body—yoga is more than a set of exercises designed to make you supple. Some techniques emphasize the power of natural products—macrobiotic foods, herbal remedies, homeopathy. Some claim to utilize mysterious forces and energies within the body or tap the healing powers of the universe.

Christianity and the New Age
Some have attacked the movement on the grounds that it represents dabbling with the satanic. It is true that it has an occult dimension which is unacceptable to Christians. On the other hand, its emphasis on the whole person points to an important truth about humanity. What the New Age *does* represent is a deep discontent with views which suggest that mystery has been banished from our experience, that the 'man in the white coat' has demonstrated all that needs to be known about Life, that our deepest hopes, feelings and insights can be reduced to something observable under the microscope. The New Age represents a profound longing that this world of the senses should not be the last word, and a profound conviction that it is the spiritual which lies at the heart of reality.

Many New Age assumptions have their equivalent within Christianity. In fact the New Testament asserts that the new and final age has already dawned with the coming of Christ. He is the fulfilment of the prophecies, hopes and expectations of the Old Testament. So the birth of Christ is marked by the appearance of a star and is acknowledged by astrologers from the East. One interpretation of the Christmas gifts sees gold, frankincense and myrrh as elements of their occult craft. At the coming of Christ they lay at his feet the tools of their trade.

The theme of conflict with celestial powers is picked up throughout the New Testament. Jesus 'casts out devils by the finger of God'; Paul declares that Christians wrestle against spiritual wickedness in the heavenly realm; in his death on the cross Christ 'disarmed the principalities and powers and made a public example of them'. So the Bible accepts the reality of an unseen world over against the material, but tends to present it as a dimension where spiritual forces of good and evil are locked in a cosmic conflict.

The New Testament also accepts the essential unity of the human person. Humanity is body, soul and spirit (see Chapter 35). Paul, one of the first Christian thinkers, teaches the resurrection of the body and not just the immortality of the soul. Jesus' healings show his concern with the whole person who is sick, particularly when these are linked with salvation and the forgiveness of sins. It is also possible to see the New Age emphasis on the 'real you inside you' foreshadowed by the Christian doctrine that everyone is originally created in God's image which is renewed through Christ so that the Christian is 'a new creation'. Fulfilled life is life in the power of God's indwelling Holy Spirit. Like the New Age, Christianity teaches that super-human powers can be contacted but stresses that this contact is through prayer and worship rather than by arcane techniques. This once 'hidden' knowledge has now been made public in the preaching of the gospel. In place of a mechanical and mani-pulative approach to the spiritual, the Christian faith offers a free and personal relationship with a loving God.

In some ways it is possible to see the New Age movement as a shadow cast by Christianity, or as the undergrowth of faith.

6 The Case of the Clogged Carburettor...

A Scientific World?

The car won't go... *again*.

Some drivers pray about it: 'Oh Lord, unclog the carburettor', or (more likely, perhaps) 'Lord, whatever has to be done to make this car work, please *do it*.'

Others will adopt a similar, personal approach to the problem, but omit God from the conversation. Speaking directly to the engine compartment, they beg, cajole or curse. The car is no longer an impersonal 'it'. It is an awkward 'you', to be pleaded with or shouted at.

But there are other, more scientific or technological responses that a driver might make. Digging out the handbook and maintenance manual, she may set to work diagnosing the fault. Opening up the toolkit, she then serves as her own God. She has the knowledge.

She has the power. Should all this fail, she *may* resort to prayer. But she will almost certainly call out the rescue services.

Battle of beliefs

I knew a vicar who could never get very far in his conversations with one particular parishioner. Whenever the talk came round to religion, the man refused to discuss matters further. Each time the same reason was given: 'But they've found some bones.'

This was, presumably, his way of expressing the idea of a war between science and religion: a conflict in which most of the battles seem to have been won by science. If science is true, he was claiming, religion is false.

'Isn't your view rather fossilized?' the vicar used to quip, as vicars will.

But the man never smiled. War, after all, is a serious business...

Science is 'hard-nosed', sceptical, enquiring. It actively questions the world. It interrogates it with the searchlight of experimental method, constantly seeking out evidence for and against its own theories. It has led to technologies that have revolutionized our lives. Having explained the world we now have the power to change and control it.

Religion, by contrast, may seem passive and credulous. It appears to accept the world as it is or quietly prays for God to change it. And religion points us away from the world we see to things that we cannot see.

Approaches and assertions

Science and religion thus seem to differ in their *methods* or *approaches*: what counts as evidence and proof for them, their notions of truth and how it can be found. Whenever religion is dragged into the dock of a scientific courtroom and forced to answer questions according to the scientific rules of evidence, it turns out to be a rather shaky witness. But that shouldn't surprise us.

Religion and science differ too in their *claims*. Allegations about revelations or miracles are no use to science. Science works from different data: controlled experiments and repeated observations. It looks for regularities in nature, rather than

> If all the achievements of scientists were wiped out tomorrow there
> would be no doctors but witch-doctors, no transport faster than a
> horse, no computers, no printed books, no agriculture beyond
> subsistence peasant farming. If all the achievements of theologians
> were wiped out tomorrow, would anyone notice the smallest
> difference?
>
> Even the bad achievements of scientists, the bombs and sonar-
> guided whaling vessels, **work**! The achievements of theologians
> don't do anything, don't affect anything, don't achieve anything,
> don't even mean anything. What makes you think that 'theology'
> is a subject at all?
>
> Richard Dawkins

'exceptions to the rule'. Conflicts between science and faith in
the past have usually revolved around what appear to be
different claims. Does the sun move around the earth, or vice-
versa? Were animals, plants and human beings instantly created
in six days, or did they evolve over thousands of millions of
years—leaving 'some bones' along the way?

In these debates the picture language of the Bible has
sometimes been taken in a wooden, literal way as a straight
denial of the findings of science. In fact a more sophisticated
view of the language of the Bible can help settle many of these
conflicts (see Chapter 10). And the discoveries of modern
scientists, together with a proper understanding of their
methods, may actually reduce the areas of dispute.

Yet there *are* differences between science and religion, and
conflicts still arise. It is sometimes suggested that they can be
best dealt with by recognizing that the *fundamental* tasks of
science and religion are very different. Religion is after all
primarily a powerhouse for attitudes. Faith is an attitude to God;
so is worship, religious love, thanksgiving. In and through these
attitudes we adopt a stance or orientation to God and to one
another, and also to the world of nature. Science tells us what
that universe is like: how it works and how it developed. It
answers the question, *How?*

Perhaps religion does something different. Religion seeks to convert us to see that same world in a particular way: to adopt a religious attitude towards it, to see it as good and as the gift of God. It answers the question, *Why?* This religious attitude does not conflict with scientific understanding, but neither does it simply arise out of science. Both *could* be true.

The nature of nature

What kind of a world do we live in? Surely it is the world that science describes. But what sort of a world is that? Science used to claim, and many non-scientists still do, that the world revealed by science was like a great clockwork machine. It was made up of an ordered array of particles and forces ('cogs and springs') working in a quite determined, mechanical fashion against the background of absolute space and time. It was a machine that might have been made by God, but it needed no divine clockmaker to keep it going.

The new scientific revolution

But in the twentieth century science has begun to paint a very different picture. Einstein's special theory of relativity of 1905 destroyed the view that time was a universal absolute. Time, he argued, goes more slowly at speeds close to the speed of light. And we must now speak of 'space-time'; for when time is stretched, space is shrunk. Einstein's later, general theory of relativity treated gravity as a distortion of space-time. Space is now viewed like a great rubber sheet bent or warped near massive bodies, with time running more slowly the stronger the gravitational force. Time is relative to our speed and our position. There is no universal 'now'. We can't trust time like we used to.

In astrophysics we discover a universe radically different from what we see around us, particularly at very high temperatures, very high speeds or very high gravitational forces. Similarly subatomic physics (*quantum theory*) shows us a world

> The clockwork universe is dead.
>
> John Polkinghorne

41

more peculiar than the most bizarre fantasies of science fiction. Nature as we usually see it seems straightforward: predictable, even predetermined. But inside the atom it is otherwise. On the usual interpretation given by scientists, there is an unpredictability deep down within nature. We cannot know both the position and the momentum of subatomic particles like electrons. The more accurately we determine the one, the less we can say about the other. So there is a fundamental uncertainty built into the subatomic structure of the universe.

A truce with religion?
So the findings of science are not what they were. The world of science is more mysterious than scientists thought possible even in the last century. It is not a great clock with each piece of the mechanism producing a predictable effect on the next. It is more open, unpredictable and interrelated than that. Some argue that that makes nature more susceptible of a religious explanation, and more open to the mind and activity of God. They add that we still need to be careful not to set science against religion, by treating biblical poetry as a textbook of astronomy or biology. But the nature that modern science portrays seems somehow less secular these days.

Science: no longer in the way?
Some would also argue that even the methods of science are not as different from those of religion as they often appear. Science and religion both depend on the judgments of communities. They both work with models and analogies: Jesus as both human and divine; electrons as both particles and waves. They both find a place for reliance on authorities and traditions of interpretation. And they both consider the search for truth to be important.

Science and religion, then, are not so different as they used to seem.

7 The Little Fine Tilth Book...

A Created World?

I'm not a great one for gardens. And gardening books terrify me. It's their effortless superiority, their secret knowledge and the assumption that you are going to work your fingers to the bone all year round. What can you make of a book called *The Gardening Year?* Why is it never *The Gardening Week?* Or even *Better Beetroots on Two Minutes a Fortnight?*

When October comes I assume it's time to make for the great indoors and hibernate until March at the earliest. Not so *The Gardening Year*. Apparently October is the very best moment to aerate, scarify and hollow-tine the lawn. Bearded-iris beds need to be tidied, apple trees to be grease-banded, herbaceous perennials to be planted, and the chrysanthemums dusted with captan against mildew. I'm also required to clear away pea and bean haulm. Haulm?

All this is music to her outdoors. She can hardly wait to leap into her little wellies and deal with the bean haulm. I've had time to study the dedicated gardener in detail. From behind the double glazing you can learn a lot.

She likes nothing better than mulching or digging until she obtains a fine tilth. Weeds seldom bother to show their heads now. Flowers and fruit flourish in abundance. The broccoli and parsnips come on a treat.

But this isn't just a matter of eating more healthily and more cheaply. I think it's more than economics. It also has something to do with getting in on the act, tinkering and moulding, getting your hands dirty; it's a kind of creativity. There is clearly a deep pleasure to be had in making a new world and reclaiming the wilderness.

Messing about

In fact, we live in a world of making. Very few of us allow our world to stay untouched by human hand. Fiddling, meddling and playing with our surroundings is one of life's great pleasures. There is great satisfaction to be had from gardening, DIY, pottery, woodwork, dressmaking, electronics, bricklaying, cooking and painting. Christians have always seen human creativity as pointing towards the creativity of God. They argue that what is a significant aspect of our own nature points towards a fundamental truth about the universe. We inhabit a created world.

Perhaps *creativity* is not quite the right word. Because even I have noticed that you don't actually create, so much as work alongside and inside the system. The dahlia, cyclamen and salvia have a sturdy independence. What is a brisk pruning for a rose will strike an autumn-fruiting strawberry as Grievous Bodily Harm. You have to respect everything's unique identity. It's a strange balance between letting it be and not letting it get out of hand. So gardeners get really involved and meddle all the time but they still have to work within the limits of their raw material.

The analogy with gardening is a useful one since it reminds us that the stuff with which we work has a nature and life of its own. The wood for shelving, the wool for a jumper and the ingredients of a cake have a character of their own. You cannot do absolutely anything you like with the raw material. You have to work with the grain. But this is true of all kinds of creative activity. The poet, artist, composer and dancer have to learn the discipline of the particular artistic form. It is even more true of bringing up a child or loving someone into life. Crude ideas of moulding and shaping which ignore the nature of the human material result in lives which are twisted and emotionally damaged.

Here again human creativity is a pointer to the creativity of God. He also respects the nature of the world he has made— both things and people. It is an aspect of his faithfulness that having given things a nature, he does not abuse it with wilful, unpredictable and capricious interventions. He also loves his world into life.

Getting in on the act

Christians do not see human creativity just as a model for God's. It has value in itself as partnership with him. People are called to be *co-creators*. They can work alongside the divine activity, playing their own part in bringing new things to birth. In this sense all human creation is God's—but at second hand, one step removed.

One of the most systematic attempts to reflect divine creativity in one's own work can be found in the philosophy of the medieval Benedictine monk Bernard of Clairvaux. The great monastery at Clairvaux became a symbol of humanity acting in partnership with God. Together they transformed the land, turning it from wilderness to the Garden of Paradise.

The abbey was placed between two mountains, on the sides of which grew grain and vines. On top of the mountains monks gathered brushwood; in the valley itself fruit trees grew; a diverted river produced power for mills, a brewery and workshops; flocks and herds ensured a constant supply of food, wool, parchment and leather for bookbinding. All this industry was an act of worship, a celebration of the glory of God the Creator who uses us as his partner. In this way, developing, modifying and improving the environment can become a religious act.

The other thing I've noticed about gardeners is how pleased they are with the results. They love their gardens. I don't just mean they love gardening. They love their gardens.

You get taken on one side to admire the great marrow, the enormous onion and the bulging beetroot. At garden centres you see people carrying home conifers with tenderness and care.

Think of the inefficiency of a God who takes forty years of wandering in the wilderness to get his people from Egypt to Israel. The American marines could have done it in a fortnight. But it is the inefficiency of a loving parent who makes it possible for his children to grow by acknowledging his own weakness and giving them room.

Michael Hare-Duke

They pour affection onto their potted plants and hanging baskets: 'Love me, love my leeks.'

I'm not surprised. When you've brought something from nothing to fulfilment, you can't help loving it.

I see the attraction.

It's just the backache that puts me off.

8 A Funny Thing Happened on the Way...

A Story-Shaped World?

Being a stand-up comic is, I suppose, marginally more enjoyable than doing ten years' hard labour. Experts like Jasper Carrott, Jo Brand and Robin Williams have had to hone their skills in a rough school. When we marvel at their slick stream of patter we forget how unfunny it is to have to be funny.

Very often the secret of their success seems to lie in their ability to tell stories—one after another, odd, quirkish, upside-down looks at life—each one a little gem following the classic pattern: setting the scene, complicating the action and resolving it with a punchline.

> *A man went into a car scrapyard. 'I'm looking for a door for a Fiesta.'*
> *'Fine,' said the proprietor, 'Fifty pounds'.*
> *'But they're only five pounds at the yard down the road.'*
> *'Well, buy your door there then.'*
> *'They haven't got any.'*
> *'Ah,' said the proprietor, 'Ours are only a fiver when we haven't got any.'*
> *'Fair enough,' said the man. 'I'll come back when you haven't got any.'*

It's very difficult not to tell stories. 'What kind of day did you have at the office/home/school?' someone asks us, and we pull the indescribable mess of experience into shape and sequence, giving it some sort of order, bringing it under control, even acting out all the parts—'I said to him, no nonsense... He said to me, you know how snide he can be... Well, I told him in no uncertain terms...'

Story-telling makes a *world* where there would otherwise be chaos and confusion. It can even make memory easier to live with.

We also spend a lot of time listening to other people's stories. They may be no more than how crowded the shops were, how thick the traffic, how brilliant the third goal. They may be life stories which leave us exhausted, inspired, disturbed, ashamed or grieving. That's the trouble with stories. They have a nasty habit of luring us into the action. We get involved; the story starts to become 'our story'. We can't stay detached spectators for very long.

Story-power

Most stories, perhaps all stories, can turn into *myths*. That is, they can become powerful vehicles for expressing our deepest convictions about reality, about the way things really are at heart. There is a story told by the theologian Paul Tillich which approaches this mythological quality. It concerns a refugee from the Nazi concentration camps who lived for a time in hiding in a graveyard. There he saw a young woman give birth, assisted by an eighty-year-old grave-digger wrapped in a shroud. The old man was convinced that God had at last sent the Messiah. For, 'only the Messiah could be born in a grave'. But Tillich concludes the story by saying that after three days the child was forced to suck his mother's tears because she had no milk for him.

Most people who read that story for the first time find it emotionally powerful. It is not just because it tells of human distress, nor because it recalls the nightmare of the Holocaust. Tillich himself spoke of its 'tremendous symbolic power'. The story seems to be pointing to the truth about Life itself. It asks the question, 'So is this what life is like in the end? Is every hope of a new beginning doomed to be frustrated?'

We cannot escape stories. Some will disturb us because they do not seem to represent what we believe or hope to be the truth about life. Others will satisfy and express our deepest convictions. The most powerful will not seem like stories at all; they will be self-evidently true representations of the way things are. And these are the myths which will create the world for us. Is the world like a Clint Eastwood film where good is almost indistinguishable from evil and triumphs only because it shoots faster and hits harder? Does Cinderella get her prince? Does Lassie always get home in the end? Is life like a Hercule Poirot mystery which will be neatly and satisfyingly resolved in the last few minutes? Will Superman rescue us all from a nameless horror? Are we all on the starship Enterprise boldly going where no one has gone before? Is humanity rising inexorably from the primeval slime and marching on and on towards total mastery of the universe? Or has the sorcerer's apprentice let loose a power he cannot control?

These are the myths of our society—expressed in films, novels, advertisements, soap operas, sci-fi, drama. But which of them are *signs*? And which are just will-o'-the-wisps?

'Just a story'?

It is foolish, if not actually dangerous, to dismiss stories as 'only stories'. Religions have produced some very powerful stories, classic myths that depict the meaning of life and humankind's place within a cosmic drama. One of the most famous is the story of Eden and the fall of humanity. If the story is used as an occasion for debating whether Adam had a navel or if snakes used to bounce along on their tails it will lose all its power.

A child watching the York Miracle Plays showed more insight. As Eve approached the forbidden fruit she began to show increasing signs of distress until in the end, unable to watch any longer, she buried her face in her mother's lap. In some mysterious way the ancient story acted out in medieval English retained its power to touch the raw nerve.

The story of Eden makes a statement. To be human is to be given almost unrestricted freedom to enjoy this world as if it were a garden. It is to be aware of proper limits to that freedom. And it is also to overstep those limits in a desperate desire to play God. But by so doing humanity loses something infinitely precious and comes to know guilt and alienation from God, other human beings and the natural world. This story is not unlike William Golding's novel, *Lord of the Flies*. This also traces a fall from innocence and the capacity of human beings to turn paradise into hell.

In this way a fictional tale can become a true story, representing the way things are. True stories allow us to insert ourselves into them. They have a habit of becoming 'my story'. They give us a place and significance in the cosmos. They help us to make sense of our existence. They keep back the waters of chaos which otherwise will overwhelm us. Life becomes manageable and ordered. I know who I am, where I am going and how I should live.

The Christian story

Christianity is itself a story, or more accurately, a set of stories tucked inside one another like a Russian doll. At one level there are stories about Jesus, accounts of his encounters and conflicts with people. These will include stories that he told, like the parables. But these incidents are set within the larger story of his mission, a narrative which begins with his birth at Bethlehem (see Chapter 38) and culminates in his death, resurrection and ascension (see Chapter 39). This historical story is in its turn itself part of a cosmic story, which goes back before the foundation of the world and takes in the end of the ages, of the relationship between God and humanity.

The Christian story ought not to be dismissed as 'just a story'. Christians believe that it is a *true* story. This is not just a matter of saying that the outline of Jesus' life is broadly historical. More significantly, the story, historical and cosmic, reflects the truth about the whole of life. It makes a statement about the nature of things. It says, 'This is the way the world is.'

This is why the story plays such a significant role in the life of the Christian community. It is this story which is rehearsed and re-enacted in worship. Evangelism is retelling and re-enacting this story, in the hope that those who listen will recognize that it speaks to their condition and rings true to their experience. In fact the whole enterprise of being a Christian has been described as a lifelong attempt to let 'my story' be conformed to 'Christ's story'.

9 What Does God Do All Day?...

A Cared-For World?

'Acts of God' keep strange company. In insurance policies they get lumped together with storm damage, tempest, hurricanes and terrorists. They belong to the bizarre, inexplicable and exotic. When everything else has been eliminated what you are left with (and it's not much) must be an Act of God.

Or they are dismissed as a joke. When David Jenkins was Bishop of Durham, people said he went around with a lightning conductor on his car—just in case God decided to express displeasure at the Bishop's latest TV interview. But very few really expected a thunder-bolt out of the sky, even though York Minster was aflame the day after his consecration.

If Christians seriously believe that God is 'minding the shop', how do they talk about his activity? What *does* God do all day?

Keeping everything going

The technical term for this is 'continuous creation'. It emphasizes the belief that God keeps the universe going all the time. It is dependent on his power for every moment of its existence; without God the whole edifice would collapse again 'into nothing'.

For many people 'creation' is only about what God did in the beginning: a once-for-all act of bringing the universe into existence. This is 'making-creation': the 'long-time-ago-creation' when God declared the universe open with a few well-chosen words. Continuous creation (every-second-of-the-day-creation) is a more powerful idea. God didn't make the universe, wind it up and walk off, leaving it ticking away on its own. Without God the world would go out of existence completely. It wouldn't shrivel up into something else, like a punctured balloon. It is more like what happens to the music when the pianist stops playing. It disappears; it does not turn into something else called 'silence'.

Of course, describing the indescribable is very difficult. Christians have been compelled to use human (and other) analogies to try to make sense of what is a *unique* idea. Here are some of these pictures. Each one has its own light to shed on God's creating activity.

The sun gives light
The potter makes a pot
The clockmaker makes a clock
The architect designs a building
The weaver weaves a tapestry
The lover procreates a child
The parent loves a child into adulthood
The musician plays a tune
The dancer dances a dance
The playwright or novelist invents a character

These word pictures tend to divide over the question of how free-standing or independent the universe is. Without a dancer, there is no dance, for example. But a pot still exists even when the potter has gone out of the room. So for some Christians all the events in nature are *directly* God's acts, and the universe has no real independence and no real causality. On this account things happen in regular ways (according to the 'laws' of nature) only because God's creative actions are done *regularly*, in an order that we can discover and learn.

For other Christians, while God keeps the universe in existence, it has a certain amount of independence or autonomy. It has its own order of cause and effect. On this view nature follows its own laws, although God has devised these laws in the first place.

Keeping an eye on things
It's the feeling that the universe is basically out there on its own that has made the idea of divine lightning bolts striking bishops

seem ridiculous to many people. God may be busy sustaining the universe but does he intervene directly in its affairs? Is God a meddler? And if he is, how much?

Is God like the father who pays the mortgage but hides behind the paper when the children want to play? Or does he provide them with toys, watch with interest and delight while they play but refrain from interfering in case he should hamper their development? Or is he thoroughly involved in their games even to the point of whisking them away from potential accidents and stepping in to stop squabbles?

The doctrines of providence and miracle have traditionally tried to deal with these questions. The word 'providence' suggests that God looks ahead and 'provides for' his creatures (see also Chapter 4). He can do this in two ways.

He can look to the interests of his world and see, for example, that 'seedtime and harvest, summer and winter do not fail'. In this general sense providence comes close to continuous creation. But it adds the claim that God 'steers' nature in a loving (but very general) way. His action keeps within the natural, predictable limits of the universe and its scientific laws. This is *general* providence. God is like a rower steering his boat here or there, but only within the limits of the banks of the river.

Others say that such a God is too remote; not personal enough. A caring God would occasionally also express his care in a more direct, unexpected (but still *natural*) way. They believe in acts of *particular* providence: a sunny day for a trip out, or a job offer for someone who has prayed for it. But other Christians argue that particular providence is just our interpretation of the operation of nature's (God's) laws. It pleases us today that the garden has rain, but God has not caused it to rain especially for us.

Popping in for a minute
Miracle is a special case of God's influence over the ways things work. The difference between miracle and providence is that the intervention of a miracle appears to break the laws of nature. (People do not usually walk on water or rise from the dead.) A miracle is an awesome, worship-evoking supernatural event that cannot be explained by the laws of science. In miracles God does something that is not just unexpected, but unpredictable and

inexplicable by scientific principles. God has, as it were, pulled a boat out of the river and made it float on dry land.

Some Christians are not sure about interventions. Intervention, for them, makes life unpredictable and capricious. A universe where God is always 'popping in' to change things diminishes the opportunity for human beings to behave responsibly for themselves. If God is going to bail you out then choice, judgment and moral decision disappear. Worse still, if God is *not* going to interfere *all* the time, then there seems to be no good reason for his intervention at one point and his inactivity at another. This objection appears all the stronger when people speak of God intervening in relatively small matters, but failing to respond to horrors like Auschwitz.

Archbishop John Habgood writes:

An unbeliever cannot be blamed for wondering why a God who can reserve parking spaces for his chosen ones could not divert a few Nazi death trains.

Despite this, traditional Christian belief has expected God to intervene in all kinds of situations. Christians pray for miracles. In this they see themselves as children approaching a loving parent. When their prayers are answered affirmatively they are thankful and their relationship with God is strengthened and deepened. When things go badly they trust that God is still in control of events and is working his purpose out. They know that miracles can't be had on demand; they can't be predicted in advance and, by definition, they won't be thick on the ground. But they don't come as the result of a whim of a capricious God who happens to feel like meddling from time to time.

Divine intervention, along with the regular laws of nature, is seen as an expression of God's faithfulness. In the day-to-day running of the universe, he may be trusted. And at any moment he is capable of surprising you.

10 God-Talk...

A Talkative World?

Language is funny stuff. And in religion it gets funnier.
Wander into a certain sort of church and fix an ear on
the pulpit and you *might* be unlucky enough to hear
something not all that far away from this...

> *How difficult it is to speak of God, how formidable an
> enterprise, how beset with paradox, a veritable Sisyphean
> labour. For God Is, is the Absolute Is, the very essence of Is-
> ness, Is of all Ises, Being Isself... (er) Itself. Some there be
> who have conceived God as a mere hypostatization of an
> idea or the reification of an ideal—this way is to pursue an
> ignis fatuus, a jack o'lantern. God is eternally, ineffably,
> indescribably, indefinably, incomprehensibly, illimitably
> real—just, one might say, So, a Thus ... neither one nor
> another but rather both together, ontic, all-enveloping,*

always, ever, intrinsically incomparabilis, *never to be confounded or confused with anything else in creation. But it would be an error of the first magnitude to conceive of God as an object, a thing set apart, a* res disiuncta. *For he is interpenetratingly and interanimatively immanent in his creation. He is the beyond in our midst, the there in our here, the yon in our hither—yes, even, if I may presume to be so bold—the fro in our to, the by in our large, the from in our towards, the far in our near, the out in our in. And yet, in a deeper sense, and I may say a very real sense, to distinguish this asseveration from other senses less real or even chimerical, his very absence is a kind of presence. By being away he is, so to speak, more at hand than he could ever be were he at hand as a matter of sheer facticity. I see you are about to suggest a simpler and more direct mode of expressing this great and lasting and irrefragable truth. I venture to surmise that 'circumincession' is the word that is on your lips... So be it.*

God-talk for beginners

In case such sermons do not make *everything* clear, we are bold to ask: what *is* all this God-stuff about?

'Theology' literally means God-talk. And Christians in the end always feel that they have to speak of God, however earthbound their language, and however out of focus their pictures. All of it is inadequate, of course. But perhaps it is better than silence; and perhaps some of it is preferable to some sermons.

In the Old Testament the basic dilemma was already raised, with the prophet Isaiah's question: 'What likeness, then, will you find for God?'

There has always been some tension between two views of God. God may be described in personal language, as one describes a friend or parent: the 'loving', 'gracious', 'merciful' *Who-God*. But theologically and philosophically-minded Christians have wanted to give a more impersonal description of God as the 'transcendent' (other, different from us and the world) but 'immanent' (intimately involved in us and our world), 'omnipresent' (accessible at all times and places), 'omnipotent' and 'omniscient' (all-powerful and all-knowing), 'eternal' (timeless or everlasting), 'infinite' (unlimited) *What-God*.

These 'metaphysical attributes' of God *can* be read off from the picture given in the Bible, but they are not the normal way in which God is described in personal spirituality or prayer. And the biblical language itself expresses the nature of God in much more vivid, personal terms: as loving parent, vulnerable and jealous lover, righteous judge and victorious king. In Bible and hymns impersonal language has also been attached to the Divine, and God described as light, fire, rock or tower, or as a wild animal. But in most cases there is a personal quality, such as steadfastness or protection, that has suggested the image.

Many Christians have stressed that the whole business of labelling God's attributes is to reduce him to something less than God. God is not an object of scrutiny, some rare and wonderful catch to be pinned on to the dissecting table, cut up and labelled or redesigned by engineers on a drawing board. God is a 'You': one who confronts us, addresses us, and is always the subject of the encounter. To speak *about* him is immediately to set him at a safe distance. A God 'objectified' like that is not truly God.

Because of the vast differences between God's nature and ours, human language that has developed to label human attributes (the only language we have to work with) must be stretched and shifted in meaning when it is applied to God. When people forget this and insist that religious language should be taken 'literally', for example so that a God who is 'Father' must also be male, they reduce the infinite God to the level of the finite humans who are the only ones to whom such language literally applies. This is *anthropomorphism*, thinking of God as 'having the form of a man'—literally a big Daddy-in-the-Sky, sitting on the clouds in a white nightie.

It is inevitable, therefore, that talk of God will use both analogies and metaphors drawn from talk of men and women, and indeed rocks, lions and doves. God is, in some respects and to some degree, *similar to* a father, shepherd, midwife or fire. But theology must also acknowledge the ways in which God *is not like* these things: the ways in which these are inadequate models for speaking of God. God, as unlimited and personal, 'lives' and 'creates' in a manner that is appropriate to the nature of God. And that is *different* from the normal meaning of such words when applied to human living and creating. This is the difference that being God makes: a difference that needs to be recognized in our

God-talk if it is to safeguard the mystery of God's *transcendence*—
God's otherness or difference from us and all created things.

Getting it right?
In the end, religious truth is always our truth; for it is expressed
in limited, human language—the only sort that limited, human
beings can understand. The truth about God, heaven and spirit
may be One and Absolute, but our account of such truth remains
partial and relative (to us, our needs and our concepts). If we
were fish, the poet Rupert Brooke suggests, we would see things
very differently—as we yearn for 'somewhere, beyond Space and
Time' where there is 'wetter water, slimier slime'...

> *And there (they trust) there swimmeth One*
> *Who swam ere rivers were begun,*
> *Immense, of fishy form and mind,*
> *Squamous, omnipotent, and kind;*
> *And under that Almighty Fin,*
> *The littlest fish may enter in.*
> *Oh! never fly conceals a hook,*
> *Fish say, in the Eternal Brook,*
> *But more than mundane weeds are there,*
> *And mud, celestially fair;*
> *Fat caterpillars drift around,*
> *And Paradisal grubs are found;*
> *Unfading moths, immortal flies,*
> *And the worm that never dies.*
> *And in that Heaven of all their wish,*
> *There shall be no more land, say fish.*
>
> RUPERT BROOKE

This is not a put-down of religion, but a gentle and necessary
ribbing of those religious people who think that their own words
can fully capture the Word. We are only human after all, so it is
not surprising if our religious truth is sometimes a bit fishy.

We haven't really got *the* words, only *our* words. 'Human
language,' said Flaubert, 'is like a cracked kettle on which we
beat our tunes for bears to dance to, when all the time we are
longing to move the stars to pity.'

Myth understood

Of course most analogies and metaphors provide us only with a 'static picture' of God's nature: a sort of photograph in words. But these 'stills' are sometimes run together in religion to provide what the scholar of religion Ninian Smart has called 'a moving picture of the sacred'. This is an account of God's activity in story form (see Chapter 8): for example, of God coming down from heaven at Christmas, or God rolling up the universe like a carpet at the end of time.

Sometimes these story-metaphors are described as *myths*. In common speech a myth is something that is quite untrue, but in theology a myth is a powerful story about God's activity which—while not literally true—carries a deeper, symbolic truth. God did not literally 'come down' from heaven at Jesus' birth, for heaven is not literally 'up there' to begin with; but there is truth in this story-metaphor as there is in the other metaphors and analogies which describe God as a 'father', 'midwife' or 'rock'. Christians believe that it describes in picture language *something* of the relationship between God and Christ, and of God's self-giving love celebrated at Christmas (see Chapter 38).

God: male or female?

God, the theologians say, is 'without body, parts or passions'. A Spirit without a body must be *sexless*, neither 'he' nor 'she'. Although the Bible usually uses male analogies for God ('father' or 'husband'), it also occasionally uses female pictures, including God as 'mother'—as in the book of Deuteronomy when Moses accuses Israel of forgetting 'the God who gave you birth'. Recently many theologians have argued that the picture of God as female gives insights that father-language cannot reveal, and that we should avoid male pronouns when speaking of a God who is beyond gender and sometimes at least substitute 'parent' for 'father'.

It has even been suggested that God may be thought of best not as creating the universe outside himself (like a male parent), but more on the analogy of the way a baby is created *within* the body of a mother. The biochemist and theologian Arthur Peacocke writes: 'God creates a world that is... other than him/herself but creates it... within him/herself.' Such language at least captures the intimate relationship between God and the dependent universe.

SECTION 2

Ultimate Values?

Most of the time most of us don't think much about our ultimate values. They're like the sitting-room floor— you know it's down there somewhere, but you don't often examine it too closely. On the other hand, if the floorboards are rotten, you could be in for a bit of trouble, so it's worth checking from time to time...

11 The Supermarket of Faiths...

Valuable Variety?

The attraction of the pick-and-mix section of the high-street store is obvious to any hardened sweet addict.

In a traditional shop sweets come in huge jars, one for each species; or ready-weighed, labelled and hermetically sealed each in its own see-through plastic bag. You still have a choice, but it is restricted. Such sweet shops are for the purists: people who know what they want. A quarter of this (not that, or the other). Mint imperials *or* chocolate-covered brazils. *Sometimes* both, but in separate bags please ('for the children', of course).

At the pick-and-mix you can have whatever you choose. Two of these, five of the other, half a scoop of that strange thing you would never ask for in a shop (not knowing what it's called, and realizing that it's

62

marketed for 5-year-olds). A bit of this and a bit of that. Anything you fancy, really. Just to try. Just two or three...

Pick-and-mix

In our late twentieth-century store we shop for truths and values a bit like that. Pick-and-mix in the 'supermarket of faiths'. 'Fancy a bit of Marxism?' 'Well, only the one... Put some Methodism in though, for Gran... and a bit of C. of E. as it's nearly Christmas... and some Zen Buddhism for Ian (looks good, I'll have a couple myself)... and what else is there...?' 'The atheist drops look nice.' 'OK, let's try some.'

A bit of this, and a bit of that. Anything you fancy really. Anything to suit your taste. Shove it all in the same bag. 'Well, they're all the same really, aren't they?'

Of course some still insist that they aren't. Some complain that mixing them all together ruins the taste buds. But we can't be intolerant of such intolerance. It's just not that important, is it? 'I do benefits for all religions,' Bob Hope quipped, 'I'd hate to blow the hereafter on a technicality.' 'All religions must be tolerated,' said Frederick the Great in the more pompous eighteenth century, 'for everyone must get to heaven in his own way.'

Well, does it work?

Some philosophers claim that 'truth' is just 'what works' (for us). So your truth works for you, and mine does for me, and there is no 'capital T' Truth above and beyond the two of us. Some observers of religion claim that religions are true just as long as they work for us. This may sound like an extreme form of consumerism. 'Buy Christianity, it will...' It will what, though? Bring security and prosperity? Bring happiness? Bring respect from other people?

A *Which?* 'best buy' in religion might judge religions like that, but it makes them sound rather irreligious. Believers do claim that religions *work*, but not in those ways. They 'work' by helping us face and cope with and live through life, suffering and disaster; rather than by helping us avoid them. Religion works by bringing wholeness and spiritual healing and salvation, by bringing purpose to our life (and our death), by giving people a sense of reality and a point to their lives. Religions work by being life-giving.

'Do you also want to leave me?' Jesus asked his closest disciples as many others drifted off to follow more comfortable or fashionable teachers. 'To whom should we go?' Peter answered. '*You* have the words of eternal life.'

Religions work in a way that it would be difficult for a *Which?* report to capture. In a martyr's death, or in the long lingering pain of an unhappy marriage or a life of poverty, a religion that 'works' may look to the world very like a life that has failed. Paul writes in his second letter to the Corinthians of 'God's ministers' as 'flogged, imprisoned, mobbed; overworked, sleep-less, starving'. In the eyes of the world they were unknown impostors, burdened with suffering and sorrows, penniless—and even dying. But in God's eyes they were *also* those who spoke the truth, lived the real life, and 'owned the world'.

But is it really true?

Most Christians, indeed, most people, take a very different view from the relativism described earlier. For them there is but one Truth. For religious people, this is God's truth. We may discover this, or have it revealed to us; but we do not invent it or construct it. It exists independently of us, whether we know it or not, whether we believe it or not.

This search for truth is a deep passion for most human beings. After we have been to the doctor, or stumbled over evidence for a spouse's infidelity or a child's law-breaking, we need to know *is this really true*? 'Never mind what I think, or want to think,' we say, 'tell me the truth, the whole truth and nothing but the truth.'

You shall know the truth, and the truth shall make you free.

The words of Jesus, John 8:32

'What is truth?' said jesting Pilate, and would not stay for an answer.

Francis Bacon

Therefore many argue that in the supermarket of faiths not all the products are worth choosing. If one of the containers at the pick-and-mix contains poisoned sweets, it *does* matter which I choose. And it matters if one reaches the part that other faiths cannot reach, or if a pearl of great price lies hidden inside one of the wrappers.

On this view of religious truth, there is certainly 'something to choose' between religious claims. At any rate, they are not just a matter for personal taste.

12 Beside This Font...

Childish Values?

A child is born—and the world will never be the same again. This mewling, puking scrap of humanity will fill the parents' waking and sleeping hours. Even when it reaches eighteen (or forty), he or she will still be 'our little boy' or 'our little girl'.

I had rather be a nappy-changer in the house of my child than actually have a square foot or two of the place which isn't covered with his toys, talcum powder, drying washing, mashed banana, Calpol... (I think).

Second time lucky?

Children have the most appalling capacity to make us reflect on the deeper things of life. It isn't just that their acts of mayhem and destruction cause us to muse darkly on the evil in the human heart; nor that parents struggling with a recalcitrant toddler can suddenly be aware of thoughts, emotions and desires they didn't know they possessed and words they didn't know they knew.

It is also that the birth of children is an event of great joy and solemnity. It asks searching questions, 'How will they turn out? What kind of a world are we handing over to them?'

Children represent to their parents an age long since gone, a golden time of innocence. So that one man on coming home from work to his two-year-old daughter could say simply, 'I feel filthy.'

Children also represent responsibility for another life, the terrible burden of being accountable for someone else who is totally dependent on you. It is not uncommon for married couples to renew the churchgoing habit on the birth of a child. It is as if they want to do the right thing by the child or are looking for someone to thank. In this way children can be a second chance, an opportunity to make amends for the past, to get right the second time all that has gone wrong in one's life.

Children are also a bitter reminder that hopes can be dashed and that, even the second time around, all one's dreams can turn to ashes. This thought is sharply expressed in Clive Sansom's poem 'The Font', which pictures parents bringing their children to baptism. Each generation brings its hopes to the 'flowering stone'. Alas...

Faith drowns: soon perish
The dreams they want;
Till they stand with the hopes their fathers cherish
Beside the font...

Perhaps, more than anything else, children give us an insight into what it is like to feel devotion. Most parents talk ruefully about the demands their offspring make on them—ruefully, but with a certain pride. Children make hard taskmasters but everything we do for them is 'worth it'. The bill for bringing them up is astronomically high but every penny is well spent. Just imagine for a minute...

Mills & Co.
Parents Unlimited

34 Pelaw Close
Childwall
Nottingham

26 June 1996

Ref: 346/9786 Progeny

Master Duncan Mills
34 Pelaw Close
Childwall
Nottingham

Dear Master Mills
Mid-majority Assessment
We have great pleasure, on the occasion of your ninth birthday, being the mid-point of your eighteen year contract with us, in presenting you with our interim assessment and statement of the charges and outlay so far incurred. Thanking you for your esteemed custom.

We have the pleasure of remaining at all times,
Your obedient servants,

Hubert and Fiona Mills
(Directors)

Master Duncan Mills,

  Dr. to

Mills & Co., Parents Unlimited,
34 Pelaw Close, Childwall, Nottingham

26 June 1996   £

TO...

	£
Feeding and nourishing as per contract (one breakfast, one lunch [years 1–5] and thereafter on weekdays during school terms dinner monies in lieu thereof, one tea per day at £10.37 x 365 x 9)	34,065.45
Clandestine, unauthorized pilferings of the refrigerator (1,879)	18,438.23
Consumption of crisps (various brands and types—956 bags at 37p pb)	353.72
Chewi-goos, Gumrotta, Tofficlag, Whipsywhirl ice creams, Exocet Space Lollies, Droolicoke (hereinafter designated 'treats', 'blackmail', or 'protection')	256.89
Clothing (stout, sensible, waterproof as per contract)	592.47
Clothing (preposterous, ephemeral, over-priced)	3,542.98
Footwear (s,s,w as per contract)	120.00
Footwear (p,e,o viz. three stripe sneakers, four circle trainers, Cheetah, Panther, Antelope, Hartebeest, 'Gimmerorillsulk' football boots, 'Everyoneasgotemillookaprattifidontavapair' running shoes)	4,362.80
Waste Disposal: fourteen gross of Supawipe baby tissues	403.20
nine gross Pampabot disposal nappies	453.60
Dry cleaning (man's jacket [twice], cocktail dress [eight times])	68.50
Cleaning carpet and redecoration of dining-room wall and ceiling	472.89
Rentarod Household Sewage and Repairs ('Your drains unblocked in a jiffy')	98.14
Transport: carrycot, perambulator, pushchair and baby buggy (upkeep, maintenance, repair, MOT)	482.68
Hired car and taxi service (cubs, swimming, gym club, judo for juniors, disco, badminton for beginners, football practice, cricket practice, train-spotting, bus station, fish'n'chip shop, Kevin's, Wayne's, Dominic's, Smudger's, Gazzo's, Gazzo's mate's mate's ('somewhere between the Leisure Centre and the traffic lights on your side of the road') all at 28p per mile	392.00
Veterinary fees for Mopsy, Flopsy and Tiddles (extraction of pellet from buttock)	56.10
Psychotherapist's fees for Mrs Mills	302.00
Psychotherapist's fees for Mopsy and Flopsy	78.20
Bottles of whisky to Mrs Mills in lieu of psychotherapist's fees (cheaper, more immediately available and more effective)	296.12
Undertaker's fees for Tiddles	45.00

Total to date: **64,880.17**

With Compliments:

Mills & Co.

Your devoted servants

Children are like substitute gods and goddesses. In fact, Edward Bailey, the specialist in folk religion, has called them 'wilful divinities'. That they are wilful is obvious; in many households it is their will which determines the direction of the family's energies, its priorities and timetable. And they are 'divinities'. Decisions are made in relation to the child. Parents cannot do enough for the baby; they scrimp and save so that she or he shall have the best. Just like gods, children require and receive 'worship'. At first it is no more than the 'oohs' and 'ahhs' of adoration. Later their every movement and word is faithfully recorded, stored in the sacred archives of video tape or photograph album, rehearsed in holy story for other worshippers—uncles, aunts, grandparents. Offerings are presented, tokens of love and devotion. Children are carried in cars and wheeled in buggies like divinities in solemn procession but, equally, like the Hindus' Juggernaut they sometimes threaten to crush their devotees.

> *We will rock you, rock you, rock you,*
> *We will serve you all we can,*
> *Darling, darling little man.*

It is easy to draw such lighthearted parallels with the result that the resemblances are not taken seriously. Yet Bailey argues that children are for many an authentic focus of religious feeling. The new-born baby is a source of blessing. Its smile is a symbol of grace; the baby has 'made its face to shine upon you' as God is asked to do in the Old Testament. 'Congratulations' is an equivalent of 'Alleluia'. Similarly the toddler is a source of unity, drawing parents together in a shared enterprise, linking them with a great community which no one can number, holding past and future together by its imagined resemblance to 'your father' or 'Great-Aunt Edie'.

> *What can I give him, poor as I am?*
> *If I were a shepherd I would give a lamb.*
> *If I were a wise man I would do my part.*
> *But what I can, I give him:*
> *Give my heart.*

As we reflect on the experience of raising children we can catch a glimpse of the human capacity for worship, devotion and sacrifice and the way in which divinity becomes a focal point of existence. The biblical story of Abraham who was prepared to sacrifice his son, Isaac, at God's command, makes it clear that in the final reckoning devotion to God must override all other loyalties and obligations. Nevertheless the nature of the child and the effect it has upon adults give us a window into the religious cast of mind. Parenthood points us towards God. Religious devotion is not a bizarre aberration, something the human race would do well to grow out of. Every father and mother knows exactly what it is like and knows this from the inside...

I think the worst thing is having to let them go. You know what I mean? We took our second son down south, to London, the Sunday before his course started. We'd managed to find him some digs, nothing special, and in a rough area. We sat in this tiny little bedroom making conversation and trying to see the bright side of things. And in the end it made more sense to push off home and leave him. He waved us goodbye and we walked back to the car. And when we looked back he was just standing there, all alone. I said something about standing on their own feet but neither of us believed it. We drove back north in almost total silence and got in late to a cold, dark house. I put the kettle on and my wife went upstairs to his bedroom. She found one of his dirty socks under the bed. That was it. The floodgates opened. She just sobbed and sobbed.

13 Home Sweet Home...

Gracious Values?

Recently in County Durham a local council official was shot dead as he gave instructions for the demolition of a bungalow built without planning permission. A plaque inscribed with this famous prayer was found by neighbours in the house, and later attached to the gate:

Bless this house
Oh, Lord, we pray.
Make it safe
By night and day.

Homes evoke intense passion.

The cost of homing

A House is not a Home, the adverts say, *Until...* Until we buy their products to paint it, carpet it, designer-kitchen it. But in fact it costs more than that. It costs the investment of value, and the hard do-it-yourself slog of lining it with memories and hopes, work and rest, care and cares.

This is *real* expenditure. But, just for a change, it is an investment with a return: an asset that increases in value. There is a West African proverb: 'There is no home that is not twice as beautiful as the most beautiful city.'

So a home is not the estate agent's details—*mod.con.; gas CH; UPVC doub.gl.; cav. wall. ins.; Ent. Hall; sep. WC; OIR £53,000; ideal FTB*—a home is the living and loving that goes on inside.

That's why we annotate (at least mentally) all those bald, brute facts about our potential new home...

71

CONNEM AND RUN
Estate Agents
Details of A PROPERTY known as

'Dunrovin',
Henrietta Street,
WORKTOWN

a large, semi-detached residence briefly comprising:

GROUND FLOOR:

Lounge (15ft x 12ft)	*Somewhere for him to lounge*
Separate Dining-Room (12ft x 10ft)	*Great! We can leave the washing up till the morning*
Luxury Kitchen (18ft x 10ft) leading to Utility Room	*Funny how close utility gets to luxury in a kitchen!*

FIRST FLOOR:

Master Bedroom (18ft x 12ft) with en-suite bathroom	*Master? What master?* *— no need to see the family before 8 a.m...*
Bedroom (9ft x 12ft)	*Joanna's room?*
Bedroom (9ft x 6ft)	*Peter's room?*
Family Bathroom	*Certainly Joanna's room!*
Boarded loft with dormer window	*Somewhere for his hobbies*
Garage and car-port	*Somewhere for his hobbies*
Large rear garden with mature shrubs and trees	*Somewhere for me to get away from him and his ruddy hobbies*

The homing instinct

Christians and others who think of heaven as 'home' and death as 'going home' are using a powerful metaphor. It sounds as though they are rejecting this life, downgrading it. But really they are only trying to put into words the feeling they have that home—the place where we are accepted and belong—is where God is.

> Home is where you go when there is nothing better to do.
>
> Attributed to Margaret Thatcher

> Praise God who is our home.
>
> G.K. Chesterton

> Home is the place where, when you have to go there,
> They have to take you in.
>
> Robert Frost

People have sometimes spoken of their religious conversion as a sort of 'coming home', even if they have never before had any sort of religious allegiance. Augustine of Hippo, a fourth-century theologian, would have explained this in terms of our God-given human nature. He wrote 'You made us for yourself, and our hearts find no peace until they rest in you.'

'For' is a translation. Augustine in fact wrote the Latin word *ad*—'towards'. It is as if we were created pointing towards God, straining in our very nature to get back to our home, to get Home.

I was on a horse once (and so far only once). It was hard work egging it on, trying to prevent it from stopping every few yards to browse the grass on the road verge. That is, it was hard work until we turned the last bend of the lane, and then the beast was off.

'It knows it's near to home,' the instructor said, as I clung on in panic. Now it was 'towards' the stable, and no mistake. It galloped home, for home was where it wanted to be, home was where it belonged. At home it would be rid of unnatural burdens and artificial, pointless wanderings.

73

As a hind longs for the running streams,
so do I long for you, my God.
I thirst for God, the living God;
when shall I come to appear in his presence?

Psalm 42:1–3 (REB)

Grace before deals

In Christianity there is much talk about *grace*, one of those jargon words which spring so readily to the theologian's lips. Indeed it is sometimes said that grace is the centre of Christianity. Grace is the word that is used for the accepting, forgiving love, support and help of God. Jesus' message was that 'entering' the Kingdom of God, his reign on earth and beyond, was all a matter of grace. This is because it is God's *gift*, not our earned reward. There is nothing any human being can do to deserve or demand God's acceptance. It is just given, 'while we were [are] still sinners'— without any preconditions.

Paul explained this by his theory of justification (being put right with God) by God's grace, which we can accept by our faith (trust) in God. Jesus is forever telling the super-religious and moral Pharisees that irreligious and sinful people will enter the kingdom of God before them, provided only that they want to, and are willing to accept God's relationship as a gift. So Jesus promises: 'Have no fear, little flock; for your Father has chosen to *give* you the kingdom.'

But it is sometimes hard to accept a gift, as it is sometimes hard to come home. In Jesus' story of the Prodigal Son the younger son takes his inheritance early, leaves home and spends it on what the Revised English Bible coyly calls 'dissolute living'. Eventually he *has* to go home. The money has run out. There is nowhere else to shelter. But going home is now a hard, uphill journey.

His deserted father, however, sees him coming 'while he was yet at a distance', and in joy and compassion runs to embrace and welcome him. Soon his father is making arrangements for a party. This is grace: unmerited and unforced.

74

There is no deal that can be struck between us and God, whereby we can demand God's acceptance; nor can we produce any evidence at all that we deserve it. But then there is no need. *Demanding* is in any case impossible in relation to God. First comes God's gift: the grace of acceptance, the graciousness of the one who truly keeps the door always open, the unqualified welcome of our true home.

> **You are accepted**, accepted by that which is greater than you...
> Do not try to do anything now... Do not seek for anything; do not perform anything; do not intend anything. **Simply accept the fact that you are accepted.**
>
> Paul Tillich

14 VIPs...

The Value of Success?

Success implies achieving goals. This may mean making it to managing director by thirty-five, or in the words of Eartha Kitt, being 'just an old-fashioned girl... with an old-fashioned millionaire'. The song, 'I did it my way' has been recorded by literally dozens of different singers, from Frank Sinatra to Sid Vicious. It seems to touch a deep chord within us—the need to say, 'I stood for something', 'I achieved this', 'my life was not without success'. People need to feel that they were significant in some way, even if, as with one schoolboy, it's only that they can spit farther than anyone else. The yuppie wants a carphone; the executive wants a rubber plant, two easy chairs and the right to use white envelopes instead of brown; the singer in the talent contest dreams of being Annie Lennox; every kid in the park is playing for England.

Go for it!
What would it be like to be so organized that you could plot out all your life goals from inside the womb before you got started. Perhaps the 'To Do' list would look something like this:

Age 0:   Must get myself born. How do I get that going?

Day 1:   Need to identify source of food and lock on.

3 months: React to tickling and cooing with a smile and gurgles. (NB: practise smile from 1 month onwards... trickier than it looks, I believe.)

6 months: If I can get someone to hold me, bounce up and down actively.

9 months: Get in a few hard sessions of peek-a-boo.

1 yr: Fast crawl!

1 yr 3 months: Shall deliver my first word. Maybe 'mama' but who knows? I might go for 'multi-dimensional'. And... I intend walking. Now I'm really in business.

2 yrs:	House-trained. (How *do* you train a house?)
3–4 yrs:	Ask questions—all the time—especially 'why?' It'll drive 'em mad.
5 yrs:	School—organize teacher to let me do what I want.
7 yrs:	Review list of friends and develop active social life.
8–12 yrs:	Collect matchbox tops.
13–17 yrs:	Control hormones, discover strange and wonderful emotions, suppress them, sort out moral values, get rid of zits, organize parents to let me do what I want, choose a career, pass examinations, think about sex, continue active social life, think about sex, ask 'Who am I? What am I doing here? What's it all about?' in an aggrieved and agonized tone, think about sex, reduce bedroom to rubbish tip, put in demand for more money, find someone strange and wonderful to spend my life with, dump the strange and wonderful person in favour of someone even more strange and wonderful, think about... (NB: this could be a very tiring time.)
17–24 yrs:	Higher education. Find job, get married, buy house, acquire mortgage.
25 yrs:	First child—girl, I think.
27 yrs:	Number two—boy.
29 yrs:	Mmmm... think we'll have another girl.
30 yrs:	Promotion.
31 yrs:	Move out to leafy suburbs. Sandpit in garden. BarBQ.
35 yrs:	Cottage in Dordogne.
39 yrs:	Promotion.
40 yrs:	Mid-life-crisis—ask 'Who am I? What am I doing here? What's it all about?' in an aggrieved and agonized tone.
41–43 yrs:	Run two half- and one full marathons.
45 yrs:	Yet another promotion.
50 yrs:	Take on chair of Residents' Association. Sworn in as magistrate. Sworn *at* as magistrate.
55 yrs:	Become incredibly active, understanding, eternally youthful grandparent.
60 yrs:	Retire—much valued, well liked, sorely missed and so on.
61 yrs:	Take up painting watercolours, photography, fell-walking, serious gardening. Win several prizes in local competitions.
70 yrs:	Lose partner but cope remarkably well with grieving process.
97 yrs:	Die, I suppose. I think I'll go with a cardiac arrest on the squash court.

Well, better get this show on the road.

Let me out of here!

Am I a boy or a girl? I really ought to have found out before now...

Go for what?

The pursuit of success confronts us with some nasty choices. First, are our *goals* worth pursuing? Are our priorities right? Our values well chosen? Second, are the *means* we use acceptable and right? Third, is the *price* we pay reasonable? Is the game worth the candle? Fourth, are our *motives* honourable? Can we bear to examine them seriously? The BBC once ran a programme on a couple who had devoted their lives to making a model train layout run exactly according to a genuine railway timetable. Their whole lives revolved around making sure the 6.25 or the 9.38 entered the (model) station on time. They were successful but many others would feel the goal was hardly worth pursuing. Commenting on media personalities such as Paul Getty, the multi-millionaire who ate off gold plates but was a complete recluse, people say 'Aah, but they weren't happy.' Success sometimes demands too high a price. 'Rat race' and 'treadmill' are common descriptions of the pursuit of career success. Alexander the Great, conqueror of the world, was found weeping in his tent because there were no more worlds to conquer. The emptiness and vanity of human achievement is a stock theme in literature.

Finished at thirty-three

The Christian faith has never had an easy time with the notion of success. Parts of the Old Testament suggest that if you worship God faithfully he will make sure that you enjoy a prosperous life. Your family and tribe will multiply, your flocks and herds grow sleek and fat, your neighbours will look up to you and consult you on important matters. Finally you will die, old and full of years, leaving a noble reputation. But set against that are the voices of realism which argue that often as not the good die young and that when Israel is being true to her calling she goes through hardship and persecution, even to death.

You will find the same tension in the life of the church. On one hand, the theology of triumph promises a church where numbers explode off the scale, where you can have signs, wonders and miracles for breakfast, dinner and tea and where emperors, kings, presidents and even traffic wardens jump at its say-so. Some versions of this creed have surfaced in the USA in an extreme form: if you honour God, your career will take off, your children will be geniuses, your wife will look like Michelle Pfeiffer and your investments quadruple. It's always been easy to read worldly success as a mark of God's approval. He blesses you and you can hear the cash registers pinging. And, of course, the churches' assets, one way or another, must run into thousands of millions.

Against all this stands a different theology—a theology of the cross. This talks about serving others and suffering for the faith. It is tinged red with the blood of martyrdom. The crucified life is seen as the true mark of success.

The key to success in Christian terms lies in obedience to God. This is the only life goal or target worth pursuing. God's will sets the agenda and constitutes the criterion by which all effort and achievement will be judged.

In ordinary terms Jesus was a failure at thirty-three. His popularity flourished briefly but then evaporated. He was given the trappings of success—crown, sceptre, robe, the homage of courtiers, but only in bitter parody. The title 'King of the Jews' was a deliberate mockery. In St John's words he was 'lifted up' on the cross, but you need the eye of faith to see his 'exaltation' as anything other than degradation. Yet, in Christian terms, Jesus was pre-eminently the successful person, who achieved his life goals. His cry from the cross, 'It is finished' did not mean, 'My life is ended' or 'The pain is over'. The word means, 'It is accomplished', and points to a task well done and a mission triumphantly completed.

Success has always been a great liar.

Friedrich Nietzsche

Success is the necessary misfortune of life, but it is only to the very unfortunate that it comes early.

Anthony Trollope

15 Can't Take It With You...

Valuable Valuables?

Possessions tell us more than we might imagine. Obviously the value of possessions is an indicator of wealth. 'What's she worth?' we ask and the priceless art collection which she owns gives us one kind of answer. But collecting things gives other messages. For example, acquisitiveness might be less about consumerism than an obsessional need to buy security or self-worth. Very often obsessions are also the means by which we exercise power and freedom. And usually they symbolize how we see ourselves and what image we wish to project to the world.

Being burgled forces the question of the value of possessions to the forefront. As you gaze at the mess the intruders have left and try to see exactly what has disappeared, you are aware of being violated at the

centre of your identity. It is not easy to say, 'Well, they were only *things*, after all.' Imagine the scene: distraught householder, detached policeman...

Can we go through it just once more. Are you sure this is the full list?

> *As far as I can say. I've told you everything, I think. (If he sucks his pencil once more I'll scream.)*

So... the video... but you can't remember the make. The television in the lounge and the portable in the kitchen. About twenty CDs and a lot of videotapes. Were they special in any way?

> *Only to us. A lot of them were home videos. (I could weep. All those videos of the children when they were little. And our trip to America. Oh... and Mum's last Christmas with us.)*

I'm afraid this kind of item is fairly easy to shift. They'll go for ten or twenty pounds no questions asked. Were they marked at all?

> *No. We were going to get round to it. (Now I shall get a lecture about home security, I suppose. Why didn't John do it when I asked him to?)*

It's as well to have them marked. And of course, if you'd had the proper window locks they probably wouldn't have bothered. It's what we call the four-minute thief we're talking about. Only interested in a quick entry and anything they can get rid of within twenty-four hours.

> *The crime prevention officer told us that. It's a bit late now to do anything about it. (Does it matter? We've been through all this three times. Why don't you get on with the business of getting the stuff back?)*

Well, indeed. But perhaps you'll bear it in mind in future.

> *Yes, thank you. (Smug, patronizing, condescending, self-righteous twit.)*

I think you said some jewellery had gone.

> *There's a watch of my husband's missing and a couple of rings of mine.*

What value would you say that was, Mrs Francis?

> *I'm afraid I don't know. Not worth very much, I don't think. ('Not worth very much'... I must be mad. Mum's engagement ring and her wedding ring... How am I going to price them? I can never replace them. Well, I'm not going to cry in front of him.)*

So I'll put down two inexpensive rings, then.

Objets d'heart

If possessions have this symbolic function it is not surprising that they are a matter of deep concern to us. They represent a major source of our experience of the precious. 'Where your treasure is there will your heart be also.' But as the dialogue above shows, the heart also *defines* what is to *count* as treasure. So parents keep the 'worthless' birthday cards that their children make for them because they touch the deepest feelings and affections. The value of a possession has little to do with its cost. This is why the loss of possessions, in fire or by burglary, often has the effect of confronting people with themselves, their priorities and the direction of their lives.

When Mr. Jones from The Avenue suddenly appears behind the wheel of a high-powered sports car, he may first of all be declaring loud and clear to the neighbours that he is a successful man with money to spare. But he is saying more than that too. For he has chosen to buy a smart car and not a new conservatory or a world cruise or an extra pension. He is telling us something about himself, perhaps that he is not quite the grey, middle-aged man he looks. There is blood in his veins and fire in his belly yet, and maybe an eye for the girls too.

The average house is a warehouse of goods and chattels. In it you will find the basic bed, table and chairs but in addition...

... freezers, fridges, CD players, rugs, lamps, televisions, radios, videos, address books, saucepans, mousetraps, telephone tables, pop-up engagement diaries, calculators, cameras, photograph albums, mirrors, potted plants, biros, magazines, cassettes, washing-machines, light bulbs, sideboards, wine bottles and racks...

Bare necessities

Are all these necessary? It is fascinating to consider the possessions which we are absolutely positive we couldn't ever do without. How would you rank this list, for example?

dishwasher

car

stocks and shares

colour TV

video

owning your own home

microwave

a holiday abroad once a year

compact disc player

When a random sample of the UK population were surveyed recently, 70% of those interviewed said that a telephone was an indispensable, gotta-have, can't-do-without item. Here are the percentages for other objects:

car	57%
own home	55%
colour TV	46%
video	18%
microwave	15%
holiday abroad	15%
dishwasher	6%
stocks and shares	4%
compact disc player	3%

Against this judgment, the words of Jesus sound vaguely out of touch with real life.

'A man's life does not consist in the multitude of his possessions.'
Food mixers, toasters, tennis rackets, sewing machines...

'What shall a man give in exchange for his soul?'
... telephones, vases, standard lamps, contraceptives...

'It is easier for a camel to go through the eye of a needle than for a rich person to enter the Kingdom of Heaven'..
... computers, carpets, power drills, microwaves...

'Is not life more than food and the body more than clothing?'
... keys, bidets, dog food, freezer bags...

'The Son of Man has nowhere to lay his head.'
... amid all these essential items, where is the space where people *live*?

Buried treasure

The simple life of the Galilean carpenter sits uneasily with the treasures of the Vatican. It is too easy for the church to preach against a consumer society while ensuring that it gets a good rate of interest for its own investments. In the Parable of the Sower 'the deceitfulness of riches' is one of the enemies which threaten to choke the word of God. But at its best, the church has emphasized two important principles where possessions are concerned.

The first is the value of a simple lifestyle. When I moved house fifteen years ago I made seventeen visits to the Corporation rubbish tip. A van came and gobbled up every single object we possessed. As it set off I recalled Jesus' words, 'A man's life does not consist in the multitude of his possessions.' Life is not about acquiring more and more objects. It is about being content with what you have.

The second is that generosity is a Godlike characteristic. A woman who broke open her precious box of ointment in order to anoint Jesus was praised by him. Some of the bystanders were appalled at the extravagance. 'We could have done something useful. We could have sold the ointment and given the proceeds to the poor.' Well, who would argue with that? Nevertheless, Jesus praised this act of holy wastefulness. Partly, I suspect, because it resembles the way God showers his gifts uncalculatingly on good and bad alike.

The general message seems to be: 'You don't need gold taps on the bath' and 'Let the neighbours borrow your car for their holiday.'

Oh dear...

16 I Just Don't Want To Be There When It Happens...

Eternal Values?

It is often said that just as the Victorians were prudish about sex so our age is prudish about death. There is almost a conspiracy of silence which ensures that the unpalatable fact of death is sanitized.

For example embalming is deliberately designed to conceal the fact that the vital spirit has departed. An embalmer's manual says that the appearance of the corpse should not be severe; the lips should be slightly parted with the upper lip protruding slightly so as to make the face look younger. But all this is achieved with the help of steel pins rammed into the teeth.

Even the language is affected. Jessica Mitford has charted the change:

The American way of death

NOT	BUT
The body	the remains
The corpse	Mr. Jones
Morgue	preparation room
Coffin	casket of rest
Undertaker	mortician
Laying-out room	slumber room
Dead	deceased, passed away
Hearse	casket couch
Death certificate	vital statistics form
Graveyard	memorial park
Cost of the funeral	amount of investment in the service

86

In its own way this abuse of language is an obscenity. But the death industry encourages the cover-up. Even the obituary notices in the local paper keep the expression of grief within carefully controlled limits. Couplets have clearly been chosen from a menu, as the same ones reappear:

> *The tears in my eyes I can wipe away*
> *But the ache in my heart will always stay.*

> *Heartaches in this world are many*
> *But losing you was worse than any.*

> *Memories are the golden chain*
> *that link us till we meet again.*

Consider also this wonderfully tacky advertising jingle put out by Chambers, an American firm of undertakers. Sung to the tune of 'Rock of Ages' it does its best to bring the terror of death within the familiar world of the consumer, the best buy and the bargain.

> *Chambers' caskets are just fine*
> *Made of sandalwood and pine.*
> *If your loved ones have to go*
> *Call Columbus 6–9–0.*
> *If your loved ones pass away*
> *Have them pass the Chambers' way.*
> *Chambers' customers all sing*
> *'Death, O death, where is thy sting?'*

All this contrasts strangely with the robust faith of the watchmaker, George Routleigh, who died on November 14, 1802, aged 57. His epitaph speaks of him...

> *Being wound up, in hopes of being taken in hand by his*
> *maker and being thoroughly cleaned, repaired and set a-*
> *going in the world to come.*

What is the point of death?
For Christians and others who believe in a life after death, the question arises: why do we need to die?

One answer is that death is the last enemy; it is the running sore in God's creation. We were not meant to die. Death, like disease, pain and sin, is all part of a flawed universe which needs to be taken up into the love of God and transformed. Quite simply, death shouldn't be there.

On this view, there is a lot to be said for Dylan Thomas' anger in the face of death:

> *Do not go gentle into that good night.*
> *Old men should rage and storm at close of day.*
> *Rage, rage against the dying of the light.*

In different ways both the organization EXIT and the Hospice movement have tried to come to terms with death and give human beings power over the old enemy. EXIT puts the moment of one's dying into one's own hand. Dying is something I shall choose to do rather than have thrust upon me. Hospices exist to ensure that those who must die may do so with dignity, making a work of art out of a necessity. The traditional Christian idea of 'making a good death' makes sense of our need to bring death within the circle of our living, to make the ending all of a piece with what has gone before.

If the idea that death is a mistake or flaw in the design is accepted, then it suggests that life is proper to us, we are *meant* to live. Death can be only a comma, not a full stop.

A different view would place death within the circle of providential creation. The words of old Simeon in Luke's Gospel speak of death as a discharge from active duty. 'Lord, now you are giving your servant his discharge in peace.' Faithful service is rewarded by a peaceful end. Death is a natural transition from life to more abundant life. Mr Valiant-for-Truth, in Bunyan's *Pilgrim's Progress*, crosses over the river of death and 'all the trumpets sounded for him on the other side'.

A third possibility is that sketched out by the theologian John Hick, in *God and the Universe of Faiths*. He argues that ever-lasting life on earth would have no shape or urgency.

> *...it is the boundaries that give to anything its shape; and there is an important sense in which the boundary of death*

provides the distinctive shape and character of our human life... Within this horizon there is the possibility of finite achievements and failures in finite situations, and consequently of the growth and development of character.

And finally...

Certainly, even if we do not go the whole way with Hick, 'knowing that you are going to die', they say, 'concentrates the mind wonderfully'. It must bring a new focusing of concern: 'What, and whom, do I really care about?' 'What *really* matters?' 'If a good fairy gave you three wishes for yourself...' is an unsettling game. What *would* I ask for? More life? But do I really want to outlive my spouse, my usefulness, my generation, my children? We desire to go on, but not as we are now. We desire to live longer, but not for ever, not here anyway. Our present lives need to be transformed. As someone has said, 'Death is not the greatest loss of life. The greatest loss is what dies inside us while we live.'

Not everything can be indefinitely postponed. Time is passing. Some choices are of eternal significance. What is done here (in this place) and now (at this point of time) cannot necessarily be rewound like a home video and erased by a new piece of filming. It is significant that the penalty shoot-out is referred to as 'sudden death'. The fact of eventual death emphasizes the importance of this present life. The experience of losing a partner, a colleague or a close friend is deeply unsettling. But one salutary effect is often to force a recalculation of what *my* life is about.

Death is the great fact of life. All our living is accomplished in the light of our inevitable death. 'Golden lads and lasses must, As chimney-sweepers come to dust.' Death is one of those ultimate concerns which shape our lives and cause us to ask questions about the meaning of everything. The Puritan advice to newly-weds—'to live each day mindful of the time when one of you will die'—may seem a trifle morbid to us, but at least it set a marriage in a severely realistic context. Death forces us out of the routine; one cannot say, 'business as usual'. This is why what is said on the deathbed is thought to be especially significant. It is less than human to ignore, disguise or disregard death.

Teach me to live that I may dread the grave as little as my bed.

Bishop T. Ken

The greatest king must at last be put to bed with a shovel.

Russian proverb

In the long run we are all dead.

John Maynard Keynes

Ultimate Values?

What is the point?

What is the point of art? Do musicians only write music to make a living? And what is the point of music, anyway? We don't need it to survive or reproduce. Why should we care whether these ten notes are in one sequence rather than another? What evolutionary advantage is there in composing like Mozart,

or painting like Van Gogh?

Art, they say—that is, the real artists (often starving in a garret, and only selling the stuff after they are too dead to go to the bank or on the chat-shows themselves)—Art is for Art's sake. Its pointlessness is its whole point. It is not done for the money or for fame, or to insulate the walls, or to be played loudly as an effective device for frightening away the cockroaches.

It is done for itself alone.

Many things are valued only for their power to create other value. Money brings security and happiness; education gives insight and knowledge; visiting the dentist may be a pain—but the end justifies the means.

But what justifies the end? Why do we value knowledge, beauty and happiness; health, friendship and life? Surely they are valued for themselves alone, and not because (when, or if) they lead to something better. It is sensible for the child to ask, 'Why should I go to the dentist?' But 'Why should I be happy?' is a silly question. Things can only be valued as means if some other things are valued as ends-in-themselves.

'Why do you want the car keys?'

'Because I want to go out with Carol.'

'Why do you want to go out with Carol?'

'Because I like being with her.'

'Why do...?'

'Because I do.'

What else can he say? It is not for any other reason, it's 'just because'.

The true artist does not care for her art because of what it might lead to, but for its own sake. Life is not valued because it leads to... (what *does* it lead to?). It is valued for its own sake.

And this too is at the heart of religion.

Religion—is it worth it?

Why sing in the bath if no one hears, or dance in the hall when no one is there? Or listen to music without being paid for it? Or carve intricate gargoyles, like the mediaeval sculptors did, that will never be seen by anyone—up there at the corner of the cathedral tower? We do it for itself alone. It has no other point or purpose.

This is perhaps what religious people mean when they say of something that *it is done to the glory of God*.

Worth-ship

And so too with worship. Religious folk sometimes admit the *pointlessness* of worship. For worship is not *for* anything; it has no ulterior point or purpose. It is done for itself alone, or rather for God alone—to give God his true worth. Worshippers do not worship in order to do or become anything else. Worship too is an end in itself.

Like art, worship is also about expression. Art expresses human feelings, insights and moods, but never adequately. It seeks to capture and portray beauty and the deep down nature of things. But sometimes depths are too deep. Art attempts to express the inexpressible, and can only create a gorgeous, heart-rending failure.

> Music is love in search of a word.
>
> Sidney Lanier

Magnificent inadequacy is the mark of the worshipper too, whose stretch must outreach his grasp, 'or what's a heaven for?'

To worship is to ascribe worth. 'God' is not just a name or title for a (the) superior Being. Our 'god' is, first and foremost, *whatever* we worship. Everyone has some god, though not all have faith in the God Jesus claimed as his Father. Paul complains in one of his letters about those whose 'god is the belly'. These are not people who worship an anatomical organ, a big Stomach-in-the-Sky, but those who value and rest their faith in their own appetites and desires. As Martin Luther put it, 'whatever then thy heart clings to... and relies upon, that is properly thy god'.

On this Christian understanding, as Paul again says, there are indeed 'many *gods* and many *lords*', for example, security, money, fame, health, family, sex, life. All good things, God-given things, but not quite ultimate. Only 'penultimate'. If we worship them, that is if we give to them the ultimate devotion that is properly reserved for God, they may enslave us. Good things can bind us as tyrants do unless we see through such 'false gods' of our own creation to God—the true, perfect, ultimate symbol of values. For Christians, God is the only appropriate object of worship.

What is worship for, then, all this bowing and scraping and singing and talking into thin air? Where does it get you? It is *for* nothing, to *get* nothing. Religious people just do it to express what is really of worth to them, what they really value. In a word, to express how they feel about God. This is to 'laud and magnify his name', it is to give worth to that which is most worthy. It is to allow God, as one theologian put it, to be God: the most perfect one, the only one who is *worthy of worship*.

To worship is to say 'Yes' to God—and thus to life, just for the sake of saying yes.

---

i thank You God for most this amazing
day: for the leaping greenly spirits of trees
and a blue true dream of sky; and for everything
which is natural which is infinite which is yes

e.e. cummings

Is This the Life?

Sometimes you wake up in the
morning and wonder if this is really
your life, Michael Aspel or no.
Something seems out of kilter with
the world, and what the experts tell
you doesn't add up with how you
actually feel. Spirituality needs to
cope with these times as well as when
the sun's in the sky and all's well that
ends well—or what's the point of it?

18 Will the Real World Please Stand Up?...

A Realistic Spirituality?

Apparently horror advertisements don't work. People don't like to see photographs of lungs destroyed by cancer; they switch off when confronted by close-ups of road-accident victims. Far from putting them off smoking or on to alcohol-free driving, such publicity just puts them off pictures of cancerous lungs and the victims of road accidents. 'Human kind,' as T.S. Eliot wrote, 'cannot bear very much reality.' Most soaps, along with Mills & Boon, present us with a nicer, safer world where Sally can have a tiff with Nigel but make it up again. Or, if this is a permanent breakdown in the relationship, she can at least find Mr Right in the next but one episode. There are some noble exceptions to this but the point will stand.

Many people still remember the outcry when it was rumoured that Grace Archer was due to die in a forthcoming episode of 'The Archers'. Real life was awful enough. Radio life ought to offer a version nearer wonderland. The 'romantic novel' does...

Pagan in Wonderland

He was obviously waiting to be asked in, with an insouciance born of the effortlessly aristocratic. Pagan felt a frisson of excitement as she contemplated his dark, brooding good looks, the handsome mouth with just a hint of cruelty, the flashing eyes which seemed to undress her even as she stood there, knowing herself to be infinitely desirable in her negligee.

'Yes?' she said, scarcely able to keep the tremor out of her usually well-modulated voice.

'Ciao.' The voice was warm and confident, the greeting carrying echoes of summer sunshine in Naples. Pagan experienced a wave of panic. She hadn't felt like this since she was seventeen. All at once she was a gauche schoolgirl again, even though she was managing editor of *Caprice*, and had come to LA precisely to set up the merger with *Unimag International*.

'I don't think we've met,' she managed.

'Fine. I'm Raoul D'Antataglio. A friend of Lavinia.'

So this was Raoul. Lavinia had been unable to stop talking about him, to the point where Pagan had begun to dislike him heartily. But now, uncomfortably conscious of the sheer, animal physicality of the man, Pagan began to understand Lavinia's obsession. Ten minutes alone with him and she would be defenceless, utterly vulnerable, a flower for the picking, lost, oh, lost...

'I'm Pagan Kinsella-fforsythe. Please come in.'

Lost, oh, lost...

Running away

Perhaps there's nothing much wrong with this kind of escapism. The fashion for 1930s sleuths and whodunnits may suggest a hankering after a nicer age and a wholesome desire for a tidy, ordered, civilized world where the police said, 'Evening all', the case could be solved by Hercule Poirot's little grey cells and the villains agreed that it was a fair cop. Cilla Black's *Blind Date* is Cinderella in modern dress. Destiny throws the fella into the gel's arms and everyone has a lorra fun. Perhaps it will end up at the altar. Billy Liar and Walter Mitty are alive and well, fantasizing their way to Wembley or Hollywood or Cannes. Harmless enough, though a teenager's obsession with one-armed bandits or computer games seems more disturbing. And the possibilities of virtual reality are terrifying. Dressed in a body suit with wires coming out of helmet and gloves, I can experience a reality which can hardly be distinguished from the real thing. Inside this world I can know total power, instant gratification and self-induced pleasure sufficient to blow all the fuses on my libido. Whoever will want to return to draggy, recalcitrant reality after one of those trips? In Huxley's *Brave New World* pain, frustration, disappointment are eliminated by the drug soma. Escape to a nicer place is on permanent offer.

And yet something within us suggests that this kind of escapism is a flight from being human, running away from what one ought to be.

Sometimes, of course, religion can contribute to the problem. Years ago Freud characterised it as wish-fulfilment: Big Daddy-in-the-Sky provided comfort in a harsh and unsympathetic universe. Religion encourages the hypocrite. So the Welshman 'prays on Sunday and on his neighbour for the rest of the week' (a slander on Welshmen, but there you are). And religious language can conceal reality, forcing someone to feel what they do not feel, affirm what they do not believe, pretend to be a saint when they suspect they are a sinner, denying true emotions and vices. An example of this double talk is given by William Barclay who tells the story of a Scottish elder with a drink problem. The minister of the kirk visited him, berated him for his lapses, counselled abstinence and suggested prayer together. The elder agreed and began, 'O Lorrd, thy servant hath been overtaken in a verra grrievous fault.' The minister stopped him. 'Just tell God you got drunk,' he said.

Psychologist William Miller argues that in ways like this religion often assists the process of denial and accelerates nervous breakdowns. In his book, *Why Do Christians Break Down?* he argues that religion can stifle the expression of negative feelings, make us feel guilty about acknowledging the dark side of ourselves and generate untold levels of stress as it insists on a Christlike perfection. But when religion operates in this way it is pathological.

Living with your eyes open

The Bible presents a different picture. One of the most exhilarating categories in the Psalms is that of lament and complaint. Here the Psalmist refuses to mouth platitudes or say what he is supposed to say, when he in fact feels the opposite. God is told to wake up and show some activity. How long will he stay silent? Has he forgotten us? Freedom to be honest with God, and know that he will enter into argument with you, is one of the glories of Old Testament spirituality.

Listen to Psalm 88: 'You have put me in the depths of the Pit... you have made me a thing of horror... why do you cast me off?... Your wrath has swept over me.' The same authentic note of honesty is heard from Abraham, who haggles with God about the minimum number of right-living people necessary for the Almighty to spare Sodom and Gomorrah and gets the score down from fifty to ten (unfortunately there aren't even ten). Jeremiah complains, 'O Lord you have seduced me... you are stronger than I. You have prevailed.' Hardly has Moses taken off his shoes at the burning bush because the ground is holy, than he is arguing with God and parading a string of reasons why God has chosen the wrong man. This is biblical religion—and it is healthy, honest and realistic.

But healthy religion not only frees you to speak straight with God; it also helps you live with your real self and accept it. Jesus is the one who asks awkward questions—'Do you really want to be made whole?'—but asks them out of love and concern. Christianity makes two profound comments on the human condition. First, you are at least as bad as you think you are, and probably worse. Second, you are unconditionally loved and accepted by God, who thinks you are the best thing since sliced bread. In such a context the God who sees to the heart and knows you through and through is a source of total security.

No longer do you need to hide. In this presence you can live with your eyes open.

19 Power Dressing...

A Weak Spirituality?

Local authorities in Britain are very tourist-conscious these days. They are always ready to push an unlikely historical or contemporary association on the unwilling traveller. Hence in the north-east as you travel south through the Tyne Tunnel you enter 'Catherine Cookson country', and a few miles later on a sign at the side of the motorway reads:

> ## The Land of the Prince Bishops

In this way County Durham capitalizes on its historical status, when the Bishop of Durham shouldered the responsibilities of the king in his huge diocese: making and enforcing laws, raising taxes and keeping an army. In the Middle Ages he was a prince bishop, a real power in the land: a power to be reckoned with.

No bishop has that sort of power today. If people have heard of the Bishop of Durham today it is usually because a particular holder of the office makes some controversial remarks about politics, doctrine or morals. A bishop's power is now the power of communication and the power of ideas. It is not the power of brute force and fear.

That should make us ask, which is the *real* power?

Power drilling

Totalitarian regimes can dominate a people: controlling them with the army and the police, with courts and prisons. Labour camps, mental institutions and gas chambers are places where a certain sort of power may claim a victory. The powerful instruments of torture, repression, imprisonment and death can bring their own type of domination. Such power can last a few years, or a few centuries. It is a *sort* of power. Is it the only sort?

A baby's cry is in a different league altogether, but it has a powerful effect on her parents. Photographs of battered children or starving refugees are no match for machine rifles and armoured cars. Yet they have their own power, and it is somehow a more *human* power. The torturers and mass-murderers are *inhuman*, we say. Powerful, yes, but without humanity. They win the battles for the control of people's actions, but in doing so lose control of their hearts and minds. Truly *human* power, surely, is power that makes those who wield it and those who bear the brunt of it more human, not less.

In this sense, then, it is always the weak who inherit the earth. And the cross that is the victory...

Wimps and bullies

The nineteenth-century philosopher Friedrich Nietzsche complained about Christianity's 'slave-morality', its embracing of impotent virtues such as pity, kindness, caring, humility and friendship; and bemoaned the Christian's unwillingness to recognize true virtue in the man of power. Other critics of Christianity might respond that, on the contrary, Christianity has too often sided with the inhumane and with the big battalions. Its pastors ('shepherds') have too often been princes, wielding a power that belittles and stifles the humanity of others.

There is a clash of values here. The Bible is not advocating wimpishness, but a distinctive and paradoxical sort of strength. The person who 'turns the other cheek' shows a strength and a power to absorb and defuse evil that the retaliation of the violent can never achieve (see Chapter 42). Mahatma Gandhi's life was more than an exercise in futile soppiness.

In the great prophecy of Isaiah, the prophet speaks of a suffering servant who bears, and so neutralizes, the hatred of the nations. Christians have traditionally seen in this figure an image of Jesus:

I offered my back to the lash,
    and let my beard be plucked from my chin;
I did not hide my face from insult and spitting.

ISAIAH 50:6 (REB)

At his trial, according to the account in John's Gospel, Jesus engages in a battle with Pilate, the Roman Governor. It is a battle of silence against speech, one sort of 'power' against another. The crowd is clamouring for Jesus's crucifixion. Pilate is concerned.

He asks Jesus, 'Where have you come from?' But Jesus gives no answer. In despairing frustration, Pilate bursts out: 'Do you not know that I have power to release you, and power to crucify you?' Jesus at last answers him, 'You would have no power over me unless it had been given you from above...' (John 19: 8–11, RSV).

Paul, too, sees himself as one who knows and bears in his own weakness the 'transcendent' power—the power that exceeds, and 'goes beyond'—that can come only in this way. In one of his letters he writes about some affliction: 'a thorn in the flesh... to harass me, to keep me from being too elated'. He begs God for healing, but the reply—as so often—is silence. But it is in that silence that God speaks to Paul: 'My grace is all you need; power is most fully seen in weakness.' Paul responds: 'I am therefore happy to boast of my weaknesses because then the power of Christ will rest upon me.'

And this insight is applied quite generally, to his whole life: 'For the sake of Christ' he accepts a life of 'weakness, insult, hardship, persecution and distress...' 'For when I am weak, then I am strong.'

Crazy and powerless?

This is a bold, not to say reckless, overturning of what appear to be almost common-sense values, and certainly of values that are commonly held. But then Christianity is very much a matter of the revaluing of our values. Paul's opponents despised him as physically weak, lacking in presence, a poor speaker. In a word, powerless. But divine power is demonstrated in human weakness. Weakness cannot hinder or prevent this sort of power.

'On the contrary,' as the New Testament scholar James Dunn puts it, 'it is the necessary presupposition of power.' Powerlessness is the place and the means of the revelation of divine power on earth.

This theology of weakness and power also relates to the wider theme of religious experience: of what it is to know and experience Christ. Dunn writes: 'In Paul's view, religious experience for the Christian is not a matter of Christ taking him out of his weakness and leaving it behind...; on the contrary, Christ is present in his weakness—*his weakness is part of his experience of Christ.*'

What does this mean? Perhaps it means that the power of God is not best conveyed through human powerfulness, for that often succeeds only in cloaking and stifling it. Perhaps it also means that we can and should revalue our own human experience, and allow ourselves to discover the presence of the Christ-like God at those times in our lives which seem *least* filled with divine power.

Is this true? Is it in our moments of weakness and failure that we are most likely to serve as channels for a power that essentially is not our own?

20 There's Got to be a Better Song Than This...

A Yearning Spirituality?

Advent can be like an ache in the heart. I suppose it's something to do with candles and November fog and the longed-for end of the autumn term and going home for Christmas. There is something that touches a chord of melancholia in the words of the traditional hymn, 'O come, O come, Emmanuel'. Advent is about humanity's yearning for something better:

Ransom captive Israel, that mourns in lonely exile here.

Literally translated 'nostalgia' means a pain for home. The Welsh word *hiraeth* captures the same feeling—'longing' is not quite strong enough. The Latin *desiderium* is not so much desire as a pining for something which has been lost, possibly for ever, and is yearned for almost to the point of grief.

What is longed for is not always easy to describe. Judy Garland sang of finding it somewhere over the rainbow, but it seems to have eluded her. For some it seems to be stopping the clock and recovering a lost youth. In the film *Shirley Valentine* Shirley suddenly stops talking to the kitchen wall and takes off for the Greek islands and the delights of Tom Conti. In the film *Educating Rita* there's a scene where the family gather in the pub for an old style sing-song. The camera moves in on Rita and her mother, who is not singing. Suddenly Rita's mother turns to Rita and says, 'There's got to be a better song to sing than this.' Exactly.

Reasonable expectations

I have a list of what I call reasonable (in other words, very unreasonable) expectations. It goes like this:

Just once I would like there to be thirty-one Sundays in a month.

Just once I'd like Patrick Moore to mention a blue moon.

Just once I'd like to hear the end of Schubert's Unfinished Symphony.

And draw a square circle, make bricks without straw, and silk purses out of sows' ears.

I'd like to see a striped leopard,

Build a castle in Spain,

And unearth a crock of gold.

And have jam *today*.

And just once, please, just once before I die I'd like to be sitting in the airport departure lounge and hear over the loudspeaker that my flight has been delayed because of a low-flying pig. (Or that it hasn't been delayed at all...)

In life we all have deep longings for what we do not have. Some are peculiar to us and our situation. Others we have in common. Perhaps we all long for a better, fuller life; for an end to suffering; for point and purpose and fulfilment—a *meaning*; for a greater understanding of our deepest experiences; for reunion with those we have loved and lost; for stability and security in a world that is passing away.

Does this dissatisfaction with life mean anything? Does it point anywhere? Some writers have tried to bring some of these longings down to earth. They have written of *utopias*, as Thomas More did in 1516 in describing an imaginary island with a perfect political and social system. But he, above all people, knew that such perfection does not exist on earth. 'Utopia' is Greek for 'no place'.

Eternity in our hearts

Traditional talk about heaven is a picture-story about the future, about what we hope will be *our* future. Wings and harps aside, whatever it will be—or might be—it must be different from the present. Life after death cannot be the same as life before death. It cannot be imagined any more than a six-month-old foetus can imagine the 'new world' outside the womb. For her what we call life and living would seem, if it *were* imaginable at all, a death and a dying.

The philosopher Max Horkheimer wrote about 'the longing for perfect justice'. This is a justice which does not and never has existed. But the desire for it enshrines the hope 'that over and above suffering and death... this earthly existence may not be absolute'.

In *The Pilgrim's Regress* C.S. Lewis created a character, John, who in his youth catches a glimpse of an island. The vision promises everything that he most desires, and he longs for it with a 'sweetness and a pang so piercing' that he forgets everything else. Lewis himself characterized what was longed for as *joy*. The vision fades but John goes home, 'in sad excitement', 'repeating to himself a thousand times, "I know now what I want." ' For the rest of the book John tries to find the island again. The story is a parable for the inconclusive nature of our experience, that odd sense of unfinished business which can afflict us and that can make us feel that 'there must be more to life than this'.

In religious terms this longing for something better and the overwhelming sense of incompleteness is often associated with a divinely inspired discontent. Is there 'a God-shaped blank' in all of us, put there by God himself? Do our yearnings point to God who is their author and their proper fulfilment? Has God set eternity in our hearts? In this mood Jews wish one another every year that they will celebrate the Passover 'next year in Jerusalem'. The hymnwriter prays, 'Bread of Heaven, feed me till I want no more.'

Utopias are attempts to describe a sort of heaven-on-earth. But is there a heaven-in-heaven? The heaven of the cartoons is of course a joke, with its population of winged bank managers uneasily strumming harps on unstable clouds, or heatedly discussing the entry criteria with Peter in front of the Pearly Gates. But jokes, like stories and pictures, have a point.

It is possible, of course, to explain all this as stemming from nothing more significant than boredom with the routine and the mundane. If life is mind-bendingly tedious day after day, then small wonder people want a bit of excitement. If everything I do is as gripping as watching paint dry I am likely to utter cosmic cries about the meaning of it all.

But the matter is not so easily resolved. Maybe the question will not go away. Where in the great scheme of things does mowing the lawn, catching the 8.15, watching the Eurovision song contest, cleaning the car and drying your hair come? In ten thousand years' time who will care that Mr and Mrs Frobisher always went to 'The Dog and Duck' of a Thursday evening? Surely there's got to be a better song to sing than this...

Has there? And if so, who's playing the music?

21 Lovers' Leap...

A Faithful Spirituality?

The American sociologist Peter Berger asks us to reflect on a commonplace situation of trust...

A child wakes up in the night, perhaps from a bad dream. He is alone, entombed in darkness. Nameless threats seem to be all around him. He cannot see the familiar symbols of trusted reality; terrified of a sense of chaos the child cries out for his mother:

> It is hardly an exaggeration to say that, at this moment, the mother is being invoked as a high priestess of protective order. It is she (and, in many cases, she alone) who has the power to banish the chaos and to restore the benign shape of the world. And, of course, any good mother will do just that... She will turn on a lamp, perhaps, which will encircle the scene with a warm glow of reassuring light. She will speak or sing to the child, and the content of this communication will invariably be the same—'Don't be afraid—everything is in order, everything is all right.' If all goes well, the child will be reassured, his trust in reality recovered, and in this trust he will return to sleep.
>
> PETER L. BERGER

This is a wholly routine situation. But Berger asks a question that introduces a religious dimension: 'Is the mother lying to the child?' He claims that the answer can only be 'no' if there is some truth in 'the religious interpretation of human existence'. If there is nothing beyond child and mother and home, nothing beyond nature, then the mother is in a real sense lying. Why? 'Because the reassurance implies a statement about reality as such.'

In this touching little scene, the parent has appealed to a reality beyond: '*Everything* is all right.' This is not just a claim about dark shadows in the bedroom. This is a claim about everything. In the end, it is a claim about God.

Back to basics

'Everything is all right.' Is it? Can it possibly be? What *is* 'everything'?

Psychologists have described a *basic trust* that must develop in young children. It must triumph over the distrust in the young child's mind and heart that unchecked can lead to a childish— and then an adult—despair: a despair that senses a basic untrustworthiness in life. Others have spoken of a *cosmic trust*: a trust in everything, a trust that extends to all corners of life.

Is this religion?

Faith and fear

Alfred Wainwright, the author of all those pictorial guide books that plot the routes of hill walks in the Lake District and elsewhere, would have nothing to do with the attitude of mind that encouraged people to fear those high, lonely places. Be careful and prepared, yes. But do not fear the hills. They are our friends; they are on our side.

Yet if you fall down a scree slope in the mist it will not seem like that. Nature will appear at best indifferent; at worst hostile. Then everything will not be 'all right'.

So were Mummy and Wainwright lying then?

What if...

The Bible has an arresting text that fits this theme: 'though my father and my mother forsake me, the Lord takes me up'. The Canadian philosopher Donald Evans writes of a basic trust that can remain even if we can find no particular person whom we can trust, even though what seem to be our deepest needs are being frustrated and 'no one seems able or willing to help'. Ludwig Wittgenstein described a similar attitude when he spoke of 'the experience of feeling absolutely safe... the state of mind in which one is inclined to say, "I am safe, nothing can injure me whatever happens." '

But what sort of safety is this, if Mummy or the scree-slope *does* let me down?

Some religious people would speak here of a particular providence, or even about hoping for a miraculous intervention by God (see Chapters 4 and 9). That would show that God at least cares, and that God will ensure that—although we are hurt—we shall not be harmed. And yet, what if we are? What of the child whose mother does desert him; and the woman who dies alone on the mountaintop, her prayers freezing on her lips?

Donald Evans offers an answer. It is a painful and daring answer, a nettle that Christianity has not always been willing to grasp. He offers it in response to some startling words of Jesus in the Sermon on the Mount—'Do not be anxious about tomorrow':

> *Do not be anxious about your life, what you shall eat or what you shall drink... Look at the birds of the air: they neither sow nor reap... and yet your heavenly Father feeds them.*
> MATTHEW 6:25–34, RSV

In interpreting this text, Evans says, Christians may recognize two species of care: two levels of being looked after. The first is undeniably a promise of Jesus: trust me and trust God. God will look after you. Here we return to our notion of a 'providential world' in which 'God will provide'. But what if and when he doesn't? When you trust in him for the bread of tomorrow, and it doesn't come? When you pray for life, and death is the only answer?

Well then, Evans seems to suggest, we have to move to another level, and hear a more radical religious assurance. Beyond the 'satisfaction-assurance' of food, shelter and companionship lies what Evans calls 'reality-assurance': 'the assurance that life is worth living because it has already received the meaning and reality which are necessary for human fulfilment'.

In other words, life has meaning for a person when she feels 'in her feet and her guts and her heart that she has been confirmed in her existence'; when she knows that she matters and is accepted.

What really matters

So *is* everything all right? Yes. But that does not mean that we have nothing in this world to fear, and that suffering and death will pass us by. It means that fear and suffering and death, on the religious view, are not ultimate. It means that their victory is a sham; that the meaning of life, which is for the Christian a way of speaking of God, is not wiped out by the meaninglessness of pain and death. It means that however much I am frustrated, however much I lose (even my life), the meaning that God bestows upon me 'abides for ever'. And what matters, what really matters, is *that*. That God has accepted me and given me value.

In a tale in the Book of Daniel, three young Jews refuse to worship King Nebuchadnezzar's gold image. He threatens them with a blazing furnace, asking 'What god is there that can deliver you from my power?' Their answer is blunt: if there *is* a god who can do this, then 'it is our God whom we serve'. They continue, however, 'But if not... we shall not serve your gods.' That is to say: even if we are not delivered by God, yet we will not worship what is less than God.

'In the world you will have suffering,' Jesus told his friends. 'But take heart. I have conquered the world.'

To see things like that is to see things with the eyes of Christ. To see the world's tribulation as 'conquered' is to see reality as it is, with God's view. It is to voice Mother Julian of Norwich's faith: 'all manner of things shall be well'.

For if it is God's trustworthiness that matters, what *is* there to fear?

Risking everything

For the nineteenth-century Danish thinker Søren Kierkegaard, faith was to be seen as a risky business, for in faith our 'subjective passion' is met by 'objective uncertainty': our yearning for fulfilment and stability by an unstable, uncertain response. 'Without risk there is no faith,' he wrote.

> If I wish to preserve myself in faith I must constantly be intent upon holding fast the objective uncertainty, so as to remain out upon the deep, over seventy thousand fathoms of water, still preserving my faith.

Faith here is not just a matter of holding beliefs about God or other people, that is of assenting to propositions. It is a much more passionate and self-involving affair, an orientation of the whole person—heart as well as mind. In the words of the practical theologian and psychologist of religion James Fowler, in faith 'our heart is invested, our caring is committed, our hope is focused on the other'. In such faith, he writes, 'knowing and valuing are... inseparable'. Faith involves mind and heart, body and soul—as does any real living.

Indeed, for Fowler and others, religious faith is just one species of *human faith*, for *everyone* shows some sort of commitment of this nature, some sort of 'faith'. Everyone, we might say, 'believes *in*' someone or other, something or other. Our hearts inevitably rest somewhere. We all worship—give supreme worth to—some god, whether it be our new toy (teddy-bear shaped or Porsche-shaped) or 'the Lord who is high and lifted up'.

But when 'our god' becomes 'the God', our faith may be said to become faith in that which is truly *ultimate*. This is true, real, *lasting* faith.

And that is religion. Risking everything for that which *is* everything to us.

22 These Foolish Things...
A Spirituality for the Times?

How odd it is—the power of a smell or a sound or a
taste. In a second it can take us back thirty years. The
smell of wood smoke transports a young woman to a
garden where an old man is raking together leaves into
heaps and cutting branches off bushes and trees with a
pair of ancient secateurs. It's late October, in the
afternoon, already the misty dankness of shortened days
makes the child shiver. But she's happy with her Granda'.
And she plays contentedly among the piles of leaves,
throwing them into the air, patting them into little heaps
and picking out those that are particularly glorious in red,
russet and gold. So thirty years later the smell of wood
smoke will take her back to that garden, when she has
done more living, when Granda' has long since gone, four
years after the miscarriage... and the divorce... The
moment will be piercing, sweet and painful, with a quiet
sadness and the sense of something lost.

Time does not heal.
It makes a half-stitched scar
That can be broken and you feel
Grief as total as in its first hour.
ELIZABETH JENNINGS

Over and done with?
Human beings can be freeze-framed but we don't like it. We have
histories so we're happier as part of a moving video. We keep
diaries and journals—documents which become history the
moment they're written and which can clutter up a bedroom
cupboard for years. Our histories make us what we are. The past
is identity, continuity, strength—and pain.

113

❏ The past is my strength. From it I draw memories of triumphs and reward. The recollection of great moments remains with me. The gymnastics award; the day I ran home from school and was hardly tired; the painting laboriously executed, but then hung in pride of place on the kitchen wall—'This is Emma's owl'; the visitor who came and remarked how tall and strong I was getting; my friends' comments that I was a good listener, 'a kind of universal agony aunt'.

❏ The past is part of my personality. And all mixed up with it are the memories of rituals and traditions, of objects and places which make up the family's story, the sense of something continuing through time, of being part of a greater history. 'This is who I am, let me explain myself through my memories.' From such a past I can sally forth, as from a castle, equipped to meet what the present brings.

❏ The past is also my weakness. It is the painful experiences of failure which inhibit, paralyse and distort. The abusing parent lives on and on in the life of the abused child, and never dies. Many adults still remember moments of harsh criticism at the hands of a sadistic teacher. (The woodwork teacher telling the eleven-year-old, 'The arrows on your drawings are small, fat and ugly, like you.') And the peer group is a savage and unforgiving world for the adolescent. This is the source of the voices which whisper over our shoulders, 'You can't do it; you never could. You are no good at this sort of thing; you are no good.' Like the nightmarish visions of *Richard III* they cry out, 'Look on us in the battle. Despair and die.' The past is the origin of self-contempt, failure, guilt and fear. We bring into every situation a whole set of memories and they make us what we are.

The past master
Like all other religions Christianity has its sacred times. The past can be made present. It is the principle of the nativity play and the celebration of communion. 'Christ is born today' every Christmas, and it is always possible to go in heart and mind even unto Bethlehem and see the thing which has come to pass. Every time that bread is broken becomes 'the night in which he was

betrayed'. 'Jesus Christ is risen today' can be true even on the nineteenth of November. The Christian past can be taken up into our present—so we can be with Christ at the manger, in the garden of Gethsemane, at the foot of the cross, on the road to Emmaus. In fact this is a long-established method of Bible study. By your imagination you can enter the picture of the Nativity. In the stable you can 'see' the breath of the oxen, 'hear' the baby's cries, 'feel' the roughness of the straw on your knees. And when the picture starts to move, you are yourself involved. An encounter takes place between you and the Christ who is always alive. The effect of this can be dramatic. It is well-nigh impossible for the Christian past to be taken up into our present without the whole world being changed for us.

The process can be reversed as well. Our past can be taken up into God's present and future and be changed. One of the experiences which first transformed Paul's view of the world was that of finding that his past as a persecutor of Christians could be accepted and forgiven by God. The experience of his past being forgiven was immensely liberating. 'Forgetting those things which lie behind,' Paul exults, 'I press on towards the prize...' It is a robust and positive way of dealing with what was once damaging and debilitating.

The past as a gift
But there is more even than this. An old story describes how in the court of a certain king a precious glass chalice got badly scratched, so badly that it was disfigured and apparently beyond repair. The king appealed for it to be mended but without success, precisely because the scratch was so deep that to erase it, even if possible, would have shattered the glass. Eventually an engraver solved the problem by incorporating the scratch into a new engraving. The scratch became the stem of a rose.

The Christian tradition stubbornly insists that bad experiences of the past can be taken up by God into something good. They can be a means of growth. The promise 'I will restore to you the years that the locust has eaten' (Joel 2:25) is not a cheap guarantee that you get all your lost property returned intact. What could that mean when the 'property' is childhood happiness, or self-confidence? It is a claim that every experience, however appalling, is capable of playing its part in our growth towards maturity.

Sheila Cassidy is a doctor who was arrested for treating a wounded revolutionary and tortured by the state police while in South America. Now she works within the hospice movement among those who are dying. Her past experience in prison, a past which she remembers in terms of fear, pain, helplessness, humiliation and loss, has enabled her to know in her own flesh 'what it is like to be unutterably alone and afraid of pain and death'. In some mysterious way God has taken it up and made it into a gift.

Perhaps she possesses an authority and a sureness of touch which would not have been possible without the experience of vulnerability, humiliation and fear.

Pain speaks to pain.

23 On Being Shouted at a Lot...

A Deafening Spirituality?

Many people are going serious miles out of their way just to tell you what's good for you. It's no wonder that we feel battered—and a little deaf. Advertising hordings scream at you to buy Knuttem Bru—the beer for men; the magazines whisper seductive promises about the adventures you will have if you wash your hair, spray your armpits and soak your feet in essence of Pommes de Terre. Politicians rant, insurance experts wheedle, double-glazing sales-people coax, teachers lecture, televangelists per-suade, media pundits pontificate, column writers opine and friends, relatives and in-laws go on—and on—and on. People are queuing up to tell you the meaning of life, cure your spots and help you grow bigger geraniums. And they are all so cocksure that they are right.

I don't always mind being told, provided the person talking knows what they are talking about, says something worth hearing and leaves me some elbow room. I am still not sure why writing in a newspaper makes you an expert on marital discord, the EU and road safety, all in a column and a half. After all, everything is so complicated—it's the day of the specialist, of painstaking data-gathering, of cautious predictions and reasoned recommendations. Or at least, it ought to be. Perhaps.

But some questions almost seem too big to wait for the expert. And, anyway, with experts there's always another one along in a minute. It's very irritating to be told that yesterday's perfect diet gives you osteo-porosis today, and that the lead-free petrol you have been using does more damage to the ozone layer that the old variety. And by the way, what are we believing about the ozone layer this week? I am sorry, but my life won't wait for the definitive comment.

Six feet above contradiction

All of which puts religion in a very shady corner. The sermon is the sharp end of the churches' marketing strategy but it often seems to be no more than an insipid burbling by a happy amateur on, of all things, the-meaning-of-everything-that-there-is. As topics go this one is likely to run and run... and yet, the treatment doesn't quite seem up to it... You know the sort of thing I mean:

And yet, you know, my friends, as I go around and have my little chat with folk—the ordinary folk, not the high-ups or the intellectuals—I find people saying to me, 'Padre, what can the church say to help me here?' And I say to them, 'Don't ask what the church can say. Ask yourself, what would Jesus say?' And, you know, that's not a bad rule for people like us, who don't have high-falutin' ideas about theology. What would Jesus say or do in this situation in which I happen to have found myself to be in? It's kept me going on the straight and narrow through a number of pretty tight corners, I can tell you.

118

Because, you know, I think you'll find that too many people these days, the media and all that sort of thing, try to make everything so complicated. And life's pretty simple, isn't it? When all's said and done. It's black and white. Most of us know what's what in our heart of hearts. And there aren't many problems that can't be cured by a little talk with Jesus. Because, you know, Jesus was a pretty ordinary sort of bloke. I expect he liked his half of lager and a bit of a flutter on the Grand National. I should think he tried to put up a shelf now and again with a bit of contiboard that was lying about in Joseph's workshop. And it probably fell off the wall as soon as Mary put a potted plant on it. Have you ever had that experience? I know I have. In fact there's a bit of a tale behind this bandage I've got on this morning. Anyway, back to Jesus. And that's my message today. Back to Jesus. When I hear them going on about AIDS and nuclear war and recession this and recession that, and genetic transplants and global warming, I just tell them straight, 'What would Jesus say?' You don't hear Jesus going on about all this Channel 4 leftish stuff. He talked about lilies and sheep and those little squiggly things that go flump. Could do worse. Could do a lot worse.

This sort of stuff is terrible—not least because it reduces Jesus to the level of a calendar motto or a Wayside Pulpit. And it blocks out the really important questions like, 'What did he really say?', 'Was he worth listening to?', 'Is he worth listening to now?'

Because Jesus *was* a pundit. He gathered disciples around him. He was called 'Rabbi'. Like other teachers, he sat down to teach.

But in many ways he was different. He taught directly—without referring to a long list of authorities. He used sharp, pithy statements—radical and paradoxical—disturbing people's settled view of the world.

He was master of the telling phrase or the memorable action. He washed his disciples' feet as a vivid way of hammering home the truth that they shouldn't mind serving one another. He mixed with tax-collectors and 'sinners' to show that God's Kingdom was not restricted to the religious or the respectable. He could use exaggeration to telling effect, sometimes in a saying ('if your right eye offends you, tear it

119

out!'), sometimes in a mini-parable (the man with a log in *his* eye criticizing the man with a speck in *his*). He was the master of the haunting phrase ('where your treasure is, there will your heart be also'; 'all who take the sword will perish by the sword') and the puzzling paradox ('Happy are the poor...').

His teaching was fresh, sharp and demanding. Whatever people felt about him it is unlikely that anyone found him boring. 'If anyone would be my disciple let him take up his cross and follow me'; 'Go sell all you have and give to the poor'; 'I have not come to bring peace but a sword'; 'You are the salt of the earth.' More to the point, however, is the fact that this teaching was all of a piece with his behaviour. As he was being crucified he said, 'Father forgive them, they don't know what they are doing.' In that painful context the words carried a message more powerful than a hundred sermons.

Earthly stories and heavenly meanings

Jesus' characteristic mode of teaching was the parable. These stories are seldom, if ever, simple tales with a homely message. They push the hearers into a situation where they have to come to a judgment or make a decision. It is always worth asking of any parable, 'Who would have been irritated and provoked by it?'

We can catch something of the style of Jesus' approach in the prelude to the parable of the Good Samaritan. The scribe starts the dialogue off with a question:

Question: What should I do to inherit eternal life?

    Question: What's your reading of the Law?

Statement: You shall love the Lord your God with all your powers.

    Command: Right. Go and do it then.

Question: Aha, but who is my neighbour?

    Story: Let me tell you a story...

Question: Which one was a neighbour?

Conclusion: The one who showed pity.

    Command: Go on then. You do the same.

Notice how Jesus makes the scribe work for his answer. He never left his hearers with just a story to tweak the imagination; or information to fill the head; or advice to be applied to someone else. Those who heard him felt addressed, summoned, called, challenged, irritated. 'He that has ears to hear' might be translated as 'Work at it!'

The parable itself is scarcely less provocative. The hero is the Samaritan, a member of a group viewed with loathing by the Jews. The Samaritans were 'those stupid people who lived at Shechem', the half-breeds who said they worshipped God but didn't do it properly. It was forbidden to accept oil and wine if they came from a Samaritan. The evidence of Samaritans was automatically suspect in court. If a Jew had to pass through Samaria he brushed every speck of dust off his feet when he re-entered Judaea. Samaritans were notorious for waylaying pilgrims on their way to Jerusalem. One Passover festival was ruined when a group of Samaritans exhumed corpses and scattered the bones over the temple courts. To call someone a Samaritan was a deeply offensive term of racial abuse. Against the background of teaching which said, 'Give to a devout man; do not go to the help of a sinner', Jesus' story was a scandalous overturning of all the accepted values of society. Jews of Jesus' day would gladly have indulged in a little ethnic cleansing. And here he is making a hero out of a filthy foreigner—against the racially-pure priest and Levite. It is a wonder he escaped with his life.

Was Jesus an expert? He was certainly different. It's the churches' fault if he has been domesticated into safe calendar mottoes. But just occasionally, a Dennis Potter comes along and recaptures that original, revolutionary, totally impractical but utterly sane word that goes to the heart of things.

Love your enemies! Yes, I say it again. Love your enemies. It is all that is left to us. It is all that can save us. Love—the hardest, toughest, most challenging, most invincible force of all. Love your enemies. Love those who hate you. Love those who would destroy you. Love the man who would kick you and spit at you. Love the soldier who drives his sword into your belly. Love the brigand who robs and tortures you. Love your enemies.

DENNIS POTTER

SECTION 4

Where Are We Going?

Things were simpler in the old days. Men were real men, women were real women and a job for life did mean 'job' and 'life'. It's tempting to look back instead of forward sometimes, but unfortunately life doesn't stop when you lose your bearings; it just goes down a cul-de-sac because you missed that diversion sign three miles back. You can't avoid going on the journey, so you may as well look ahead...

24 Life Maps...

A Hopeful Journey?

It's the train travelling that gets you. I don't mean the delays and the overcrowding, and the hiss from the Walkman in the ear of the youth opposite, or even the aged yuppie with his laptop *and* mobile phone (a bit over the top for standard class, surely?).

I mean the *journey*.

It's different by car. Then you see mainly roads and other cars, and you have to concentrate on them (even if someone else is driving). Houses, towns, people are also there; but they only have walk-on parts. They are not the main actors.

On the train they are centre stage. The railway comes *behind* their houses, often raised up so that it can see better, like the best seats in the theatre. And

having nothing better to do you look. You look at the houses, at the gardens and back yards. And, as dusk falls, you cannot help but peer directly into the illuminated innards of domestic lives.

Here is a table set for tea. In the next house only an empty room, but a light in the bathroom. Then a TV set flickering in the corner. Next one along has a throng of children and parents at someone's birthday party, spilling out on to a patio with its cunningly tethered balloons.

A couple of seconds or less is all the train allows to each life, each family: each complex of unique individuals and relationships, loves and despairs, pains and joys. And then it has gone. And the next one. And the next...

There are so many different people. So many different experiences. And my journey takes me past them all—one glimpse and I'm away. No time even to wave. The song speaks of seeing someone for a moment 'passing by' and adds 'and yet I love her till I die'. Yes, that is possible—and terrible.

Training for life

Train journeys, in which we sweep past people's lives, remind me that my life is moving too. It would be nice to think that *it* also had a direction, and a destination. But at any rate it certainly moves on. And at a fast rate.

Some of my relationships and experiences and commitments seem hardly to last longer than a half-wave from a train. One glance, and they've gone. To live is to move. But I wish, sometimes, that it would just slow down.

Sometimes, I even wish that I could get off.

Journals of journeying

The metaphor that treats life as a journey comes naturally to us. Life has a beginning, a sort of movement and a kind of direction. It has its ups and downs and twists and turns. And it has a definite end: which may or may not be seen as an 'arrival' or 'goal', or even as a new beginning. We call that end death.

In recent years psychologists have written a great deal about 'the journey' of human life. They have described certain moments of our life as 'passages' and 'movements'. We find this useful, because in the dangerous and unknown terrain of life we are sometimes desperate to find our bearings, to catch a glimpse on a map of what to expect next.

John Bunyan, writing in prison in 1672, described the life of the Christian as a journey, a 'Pilgrim's Progress' from the City of Destruction to the Heavenly City *via* the Slough of Despond, the Hill of Difficulty, the House Beautiful, Vanity Fair and other halts along the way.

Bunyan was echoing a very ancient tradition: one which starts in the first book of the Bible. The history of Israel begins with a journey, as Abraham is called by God out of the city of Ur, to travel to a new land where his descendants will become a great nation. Eventually they get there, but their travels have in fact hardly yet begun. They migrate to Egypt, where they are later enslaved. But God 'brings them out of Egypt' in an exodus—or escape—that leads to a trip to Mount Sinai, and then out across the deserts back to the Promised Land.

Centuries later, history is repeated when Israel is overrun by one Empire after another and the Jews are transported to Assyria, or (later) to Babylonia—the Exile, from which some returned. Finally they are scattered across the Roman Empire and eventually, as 'wandering Jews', throughout Europe—and the Promised Land is inhabited by others.

On all these journeys the people learned what it was to be a people of God. On the road: on the move, as it were.

Jesus is one of these people, one 'who has nowhere to lay his head'. He called his disciples not to believe a, b and c, or to do x, y and z. Not at first, anyway. At first he called them simply and solely *to follow*. On the road, following their rabbi, he teaches them with his face set toward Jerusalem, where he will die. They stumble behind, terrified, learning what it is to follow 'the Way'—the road of Christian discipleship.

'To travel hopefully is a better thing than to arrive,' wrote Robert Louis Stevenson. But to travel hopefully suggests that we are travelling somewhere. A journey is not an aimless ramble. It has a direction, a purpose and a goal. If life is to be seen like that, we need a sense of direction.

Christian hope and Christian imagination help. 'What is life for?' is too big a question. 'What is my life for?' is more personal, and answerable.

As they travelled along they met a man on the road who said to him, 'I will follow you wherever you go.' Jesus answered, 'Foxes have holes and the birds of the air have nests, but the Son of Man has nowhere to lay his head.'

Another to whom he said, 'Follow me', replied, 'Let me go and bury my father first.' But he answered, 'Leave the dead to bury their dead; your duty is to go and spread the news of the kingdom of God.'

Another said, 'I will follow you, sir, but first let me go and say goodbye to my people at home.' Jesus said to him, 'Once the hand is laid on the plough, no one who looks back is fit for the kingdom of God.'

Luke 9:57–62 (JB)

The Christian disciple, who strains to see ahead the figure of Jesus walking the same road, suggests a very personal answer: 'My life is about following Jesus along this (my) particular road.'

This is theological travelling: journeying to Jerusalem—the place of death and resurrection—by living in the footsteps of Christ.

25 Life is Like a Toothache...

A Suffering Journey?

> Life is a tragedy wherein we sit as spectators for a while and then act out our part in it.
>
> Jonathan Swift

> If it's not hurting, it's not working.
>
> Any third Government spokesperson

> Life is like a toothache.
>
> Patrick Burke

The big things *and* the little things get us down. Cheerful thoughts for a dry season? There's always *something*. And even the little things seem big at two o'clock in the morning...

Wife: [sternly] *Will you keep still and let me have some bedding on my side? You're supposed to sleep under the quilt, not wrap it round you. If we get divorced you'll want custody of that duvet, won't you?*

Husband: [plaintively] *I can't go to sleep.*

Wife: *Of course you can't—dozing all night in front of the box. I don't know why you insist on watching the late-night horror movies. You're asleep before the first defenceless female has gone out into the night alone to investigate the strange noises. Keep still.*

Husband: *I'm worried about the loft. I think it's got dry rot. The house is falling down. We've got galloping fungus in the rafters. It will have collapsed by the morning and we'll be buried in the fall-out of spores.*

Wife: *Oh, good grief. Why?*

Husband: *[exasperatedly] How do I know why? God doesn't love us anymore, I suppose. The great Ernie in the sky has whirred, clicked and computed that it's our turn to be dropped in it. Again. I don't know why.*

Wife: *I don't mean 'Why, what is the meaning of it all?' I mean 'Why do you think we've got dry rot?'*

Husband: *I was up there before tea and I saw some white stuff in a corner.*

Wife: *'White stuff.'*

Husband: *Yes.*

Wife: *'In a corner?'*

Husband: *Yes!*

Wife: *[sarcastically] Not very much of a botanist, are you? Or an architect? Do try to be more technical. White what? Mycelium, fruiting body, exoconidia, obligate saprobe? In a corner of what? Purlin, king-post, rafter?*

Husband: *Yes, no—I don't know. Does it matter?*

Wife: *Go to sleep.*

Husband: *[worried] We're going to be ruined. The building society will repossess the house. We'll have to sell the children...*

Wife: *Go to sleep.*

Husband: *[hysterically] I saw it, I tell you. White threads—on that (er) vertical bit by the trapdoor. Great tentacles of disaster spreading like wild fire....*

Wife: *GO TO SLEEP! [Quietly] I snagged my cardi on it last time I was up there.*

Husband: *What? Are you sure? O thank God. Thank God. Thank you, God. I'll send that cheque to Christian Aid, I promise. [More calmly] What were you up there for, anyway?*

Wife: *Oh, someone was round from some nature conservancy group. The loft is full of breeding bats.*

Daily we learn of distant disasters—'Thousands made homeless by floods in Pakistan', 'Death toll rises in Rwanda'. Every year we experience one that is closer to home and friends and family. Each time we cannot help asking ourselves: 'Why them?'; 'Why me?'

Finding fault

In 1755 the city of Lisbon was devastated by an earthquake. On the morning of All Saints Day the faithful were crushed or burnt alive at their devotions. Some put this down to God's displeasure at the sinfulness of the Portuguese. Voltaire thought differently:

> *Say ye o'er that quivering mass of flesh,*
> *God is avenged, the wage of sin is death?*
> *What crime, what sin, had those young hearts conceived?...*

Although Christians have sometimes tried to explain human suffering as a punishment for human sin—and frankly the Bible itself at times seems to support such a view—the idea of God giving us what we deserve, until it hurts, seems untrue to the facts and unworthy of God. And the Bible, again at times, agrees:

> *As he went on his way Jesus saw a man who had been blind from birth. His disciples asked him. 'Rabbi, why was the man born blind? Who sinned, this man or his parents?' 'It is not that he or his parents sinned,' Jesus answered, 'he was born blind so that God's power might be displayed in curing him'*
>
> JOHN 9:1–3, REB

But is that any better an excuse for suffering? So why *does* it happen? Why them? Why me?

131

Inevitable or intentional?

Is it that it just happens, and there is no answer to the question *Why*? Is suffering just chance: a randomness built into the cosmos which inevitably sometimes produces an earthquake here, or a cancer growth there?

The theologian Austin Farrer wrote that a universe made up of interacting matter is bound to lead to interference and conflict from the level of atoms right up to galaxies; everywhere clashes, violent crashes. This, Farrer said, is 'the grand cause of physical evil'. You could only get rid of that evil by having a creation without any matter in it. But what sort of a universe would that be? Very different, certainly.

Or is suffering more *intended* than that argument suggests? Surely God does not intend *this* person to suffer in *that* way, but he clearly does allow pain and suffering in his world. What possible reason could there be for it? The only pain that *we* are justified in inflicting on one another—or 'allowing'—is as a painful means to a better end: in the dentist's chair, under the surgeon's knife, or on the obstetric couch. Paul suggested once that the pain of creation was a bit like that:

> *Up to the present, as we know, the whole created universe in all its parts groans as if in the pangs of childbirth.*

Is all this suffering in the world somehow unavoidable *if* we are to evolve, grow and mature into the glorious liberty of the children of God?

Some have asked, what sort of people would we grow up to be in a world without any suffering? Such a world would be painless, sure enough; and that would be a welcome relief. But it would, as the theologian John Hick puts it, 'involve no need for exertion, no kind of challenge, no problems to be solved or difficulties to be overcome'.

Such a heaven-on-earth would include nothing to avoid and nothing to seek. We should have no need there for either compassion or courage, there would be no call for co-operation or mutual help. 'By eliminating the problems and hardships... life would become like a reverie in which, delightfully but aimlessly, we should float and drift at ease.'

We might think that that sounds good. But does it really? Innocent of temptation, immune from hardship, unchallenged by evil, would we even be human—let alone good—in this perfectly painless world?

The point of suffering

Perhaps it is only in the kind of world that we already have, where evil has to be met and those who suffer need to be cared for, loved and healed, that we can develop the virtue of compassion and the love of that which is good. It is just this sort of messy, painful world of suffering that has the potential to draw from us the response of a caring spirit. We would not fight alongside Christ if there were no battle to be waged.

And as for *fairness*... Well life is certainly not 'fair', and suffering is rarely 'just'. But if the world was without it altogether, would we become *better*—more compassionate, caring, courageous—or just more *contented*?

The world can be a hell of a place, and the suffering that comes to us and others mostly seems quite undeserved: uncalled for, gratuitous. But, as the philosopher Anthony O'Hear has confessed: 'many of [our] most noble, dignified and sympathetic... responses to the suffering and tragedy of existence are responses precisely to the apparent gratuity of it all'.

Life, for all its diseases and famines, at least offers us both the chance and the challenge of living to make it less of a hell for others, and so for ourselves. That possibility is also built into the world.

In the end...

Suffering need never be the last word. The last word sounds more like 'hope'.

Hope is the courage to face life—and death—trusting that no disaster is in the end irredeemable, or utterly pointless. Paul's reason for such hope was that there is 'nothing in death or life,.... in the world as it is or the world as it shall be,.... nothing in all creation that can separate us from the love of God in Christ Jesus'. For, 'if God is on our side, who is against us?'

On that view, despair, failure, incoherence, tragedy or loss cannot be the end of any story.

26 It's Only Human...

A Sinful Journey?

Scientists in the USA have managed to patent the first genetically engineered animals to be produced. They are white mice with their genetic codes altered just a little. The result of this rearrangement is that each mouse is born with cancer and is guaranteed to die helpfully within ninety days. This has proved an enormously profitable move and the mice are currently selling to the research industry at the equivalent of around £56 each.

Is it just a sentimental love of animals that provokes a shudder of revulsion? Or has this news report taken on the character of a parable? Once again humankind with enormous ingenuity and technical sophistication has received part of God's creation and delicately,

THE MOST DANGEROUS ANIMAL IN THE WORD

carefully inserted death into it. Once again our actions point to a darkness within us.

At Slimbridge Wildfowl Centre there used to be a large picture displayed at one end of the entrance hall. Even a long way away it was still easy to read the caption. 'The most dangerous animal in the world,' it said. Intrigued by the words visitors would approach the picture with curiosity and anticipation. A pity really—because there was no photograph of a killer shark or a maddened rhinoceros. Just a mirror.

It's dark inside

We dislike being framed in this way. It is more comfortable to point to the darkness in others, particularly if they make something of an exhibition of it. So in a strange way the excesses of Hitler's death camps, Pol Pot's and Stalin's purges, Saddam Hussein's gassing of the Kurds, Serbian and Croatian atrocities in the name of ethnic cleansing are all vaguely comforting. They permit us to feel outrage and indignation, and even the luxury of despairing of the human race. In the same way the evidence of human rights abuse collected by Amnesty International can sometimes constitute a respectable form of pornography. We read the details of the torture with disgust and fascination.

But something stirs nevertheless. What the papers call 'mindless violence' is not utterly unintelligible to us. A perfectly respectable businessman was once about to reverse into a parking space when the car behind nipped in and took it. Slowly and deliberately he continued the manoeuvre until his car crushed the headlight, wing and front door of the vehicle behind him. When he was asked at the trial what he felt like at that moment, he said, 'Bloody marvellous.'

Frankly, it's nice to be nasty. It's fun to exercise power over others, to mould and shape and manipulate. Who wants to be Pollyanna when Cruella de Vile is on offer? It's the wolf who gets all the best lines, not Little Red Riding Hood.

All over the country pleasant, mild-mannered old ladies destroy their daughters' lives with a lethal combination of blackmail and extortion. Sociable, life-and-soul-of-the-golf-club bosses push secretaries to the verge of breakdown. Perky, intelligent children pull the wings off flies and burn ants with magnifying glasses. Even where we ourselves are concerned, there is something not entirely distasteful about the misfortunes of our friends. We are nasty enough to think, 'heh, heh, heh', even when commiserating.

And having started small, why stop? It is not difficult to find examples of human nastiness. The novel *Lord of the Flies* shows how a group of boys stranded on a desert island after a plane crash can turn what is a Paradise into a Hell, complete with flames. But the appearance of a Royal Navy cruiser at the end of the book reminds the reader that what little boys can do, adults can do much better. Bullying turns to torture; pulling wings off flies turns to needless experimentation on live animals; vandalizing phone boxes turns to the dumping of toxic waste. And so on.... until the beast in humanity is revealed in all its horror.

Your disobedient servant

Christians have tried to account for the darkness of the human heart by means of a technical term: 'sin'. Properly understood sin is an offence against God—it is playing God, rebelling against one's created condition and acting as if one were God. The story of Lucifer, son of the morning star, the 'light bearer', first among all the hosts of heaven, is an example of the essence of sin. Possessing almost everything, he lusted after the one thing which was out of reach—to be in God's place. Expelled from Heaven and banished from the face of God, Lucifer—the 'Fallen Angel'—is a spectacular paradigm of the heart of sin and its appalling consequences.

More well known, though probably more misunderstood, is the story of Adam and Eve. Set in a garden where everything is perfect and where everything is created for their enjoyment, only one fruit is forbidden. But the thought that when they eat of this fruit they will be like God is enough. They eat, their eyes are opened, guilt and fear come into the world and the perfect relationship which they have with God is shattered. And so they lose that first innocence and the garden of delights, condemned to wander in a wilderness of their own making, in a far country, 'East of Eden'.

Such stories show that sin is not, according to the Christian way of thinking, to be reduced to the breaking of old-fashioned taboos, or lack of education or faulty upbringing. Its *root* cause does not lie in social structures and a poor environment, though they can make the operation of sin more obviously visible. It is not at all the same thing as crime, which is defined in relation to the law. It may show itself in 'man's inhumanity to man', but that is not its essence. And it has next to nothing to do with 'My Wedding Night of Terror', 'Vice Queen's Twelve Years of Hell' and 'Midnight Sex Orgy in Old Folk's Home'. The root of sin is rebellion. Theologians often describe it as separation from God, a life alienated from him and determined to go its own way without reference to him.

William Golding's *Pincher Martin* is a terrifying picture of the human state. Shipwrecked on a rock far out to sea, deafened by the storm, battered by the waves, Martin is intransigent in his rebellion. Painfully he stands upright and shrieks everlasting defiance into the face of God: 'I shit on your compassion.'

Deep down, we are all capable of that. 'There, but for the grace of God, go I.'

So: 'Lord, have mercy on me, a sinner...'

27 The Devil Rides Out...

A Fearful Journey?

In the autumn of 1991 the Meadowell estate, part of a
run-down area in Newcastle upon Tyne, erupted into
violence. According to witnesses the immediate cause
of the orgy of destruction which left the area
devastated and burning was simple. Some youths had
been killed while driving away in a stolen car from
pursuing police. 'These were not joyriders,' a relative of
one of the victims explained angrily, 'they were genuine
professional thieves setting up a job.' The response
was swift and uncontrolled. That night large numbers
of youths and children went on the rampage.
Meadowell burned and for a time the situation was
beyond the control of the police.

The interpretations of the violence varied
considerably. The Archbishop of Canterbury pointed out
the damaging effects of long-term urban deprivation
and structures of oppression; a local vicar put it all
down to sin. What was ironic about the riot was the
fact that the damage was a self-inflicted wound. People
destroyed the area in which they themselves lived. But
at the same time eyewitnesses noticed a sense of
excitement in the air. Destruction carried its own
reward; logic and rationality had little to offer to young
men intent on wreaking havoc.

It is such experiences which make people think that
the category of *the demonic* is still useful and ought not
to be relegated to the Middle Ages. Meadowell was
seen by some as an outbreak of evil—malign,
irrational, and ultimately self-destructive. Could the
wilderness which faced the shocked nation on its

morning television screens really be put down just to the anger of disaffected youths? Was there in addition another power at work, profoundly evil, using the human agents as its tools and instruments? What seemed like 'mindless violence' suggested to many altogether too violent and active a Mind.

Old Nick or Satan?

Our world tends to handle the demonic in two contrasting ways. It is, and probably always has been, a source of amusement. The pantomime devil in red tights and a toasting fork is a figure of fun. There are jokes about waking up in hell and not being able to get near the fire for vicars. C. S. Lewis produced a string of profound observations about the nature of evil in his *Screwtape Letters*, but the format is a humorous one in which a senior devil writes acid advice to a bungling junior. When the Chief Constable of Manchester, James Anderton, seemed to profess an excessively accurate knowledge of the Devil and his *modus operandi* the tabloids split their sides and the quality papers tittered condescendingly. When three bored housewives in *The Witches of Eastwick* ask for a little excitement in their lives, Jack Nicholson appears as the horny answer to every bored housewife's prayer.

But that is not the end of the story. The demonic is also a topic which exercises a dark fascination. The *Omen* films are not situation comedies. Ouija boards have been known to lead those who play with them into trauma and hysteria. Hallowe'en used to be seen as a harmless prank. Now educational bodies attack it as dangerous and schools have virtually banished the ghoulish masks from the curriculum, leapfrogging from harvest festivals into Christmas art and craft. Churches are periodically vandalized and police identify the marks of a Black Mass.

Many of our superstitions have the devil to thank for their existence. 'Bless you' after a sneeze will stop him sneaking into your body while your soul is temporarily absent. Not walking under a ladder means that you will not bump into him, for ever since the body of Jesus was taken down from the cross, his satanic majesty has lurked under ladders.

More disturbing still are the reports, more frequent than in the past, of satanic rituals linked with the systematic sexual abuse of children. A television exposé of a satanic ring in Nottingham claimed that young children were taken in a half-drugged state to cellars beneath Wollaton Hall and there forced to participate in obscene and blasphemous practices. From time to time exorcisms make the national newspapers. There are accounts of disturbed people who behave in violent, destructive ways, exhibiting superhuman strength, resisting normal methods of counselling, reacting with fury to the name of Christ and apparently able to change both persona and voice. These frightening manifestations have caused many to re-emphasize the idea of an active, malicious and personal power of evil.

Principalities and powers

Certainly this is the world-view of the New Testament. In the Gospels Jesus does battle with the powers of evil. He overcomes Satan's temptations in the wilderness and, in his own phrase, 'binds the strong man'. Exorcisms mark the progress of his ministry and are explained as the signs of the Kingdom of God. 'If I by the finger of God cast out demons,' he declares, 'then know that the Kingdom of God has come among you.' Satan is seen as active in the events of Jesus' last week of life. Judas is used as his instrument; Peter is 'sifted like wheat'. The prince of this world and the powers of darkness have their moment at Christ's trial, torture and crucifixion but in the manner of his dying and his resurrection Satan's power is broken and a cosmic victory won.

For Paul too the principalities and powers are real. The Christian 'wrestles' against them. Satan tries to thwart Paul in his work, 'masquerading as an angel of light', but the apostle lives in the faith that 'the God of peace will crush Satan' beneath the Christian's feet. Certainly Christ's death and resurrection mark the defeat of Satan so that 'neither angels nor principalities nor powers... can separate' the believer 'from the love of God which is in Christ Jesus'.

Deliver us from evil

Contemporary Christians react in different ways to these passages. For some they are to be understood in the most straightforward way, as pointing to a dimension of spiritual reality which is to be taken with the utmost seriousness. Others see them as mythological or symbolic, pointing vividly to the reality of evil and to the way in which it sometimes seems to be more than the sum of its human parts or to assume superhuman proportions. Berger, the sociologist, writes of the 'evil incarnate' in Eichmann and other Nazi war criminals. Such evil offends our sense of what may be properly called human. It seems to cry out for a curse of eternal dimensions; it seems to require something which we might call damnation.

The category of the demonic may also make sense for us of strange cases where individuals seem to be 'driven' or 'possessed' by forces beyond their control. Again, groups of people seem sometimes to be afflicted by a kind of committee madness. Perfectly sensible individuals make decisions in concert that each will bitterly regret later. Crowds too can behave like a beast with many heads, and the individual moral sense be submerged in the collective desire to hurt or destroy. And the state can make demands on its members which are the prerogative only of God. When the state (or the church for that matter) behaves like God then it is demonic. Amnesty International reports instances of cruelty which beggar imagination—a boy barbecued alive by soldiers, a nun raped with an electric cattle prod.

In the face of such monstrous evil our faith in human rationality, tolerance, the use of argument and weighing of evidence breaks down. It's as though, in the shadows, we can just make out the shape of the horns...

28 Asking for the Moon...

A Prayerful Journey?

In the middle of a glum morning spent discovering a mountain of jobs still left over from yesterday's glum afternoon, I suddenly remember that I have been selected to go forward to a *Reader's Digest* prize draw. 'Out of very few' in the same county.

How much was it again? A lot: enough to retire on. There were some suggestions as to how to spend the money, and still have plenty left over to warrant an unsolicited interview with the bank's investment adviser. One was 'a holiday of a lifetime', I recall. None of them was 'a gift to the charity of your choice', but I suppose that wouldn't have had the same pull.

Then I'd be able to tell several people what I really thought of them (about forty-seven at the last count). Being rich—well, all right, financially secure—would do wonders for one's outspokenness. Of course, they mustn't know that I'd won the money... It would have to be my smug, self-satisfied, secret nest-egg... I wonder if you can be anonymous as a *Reader's Digest* winner? If they insist on a photo I shall adopt a disguise, and deliberately misspell my name...

I've never had a new car, not *new* new. That might be fun, or would I just worry even more about getting it scratched? Move house, though. Yes, sir. Detached this time, *very* detached; so I could turn up the stereo without sour looks next morning from Mrs Next-Door. And pay someone else to decorate it. *And* to do the gardening.

I wonder how many people do go forward to the Prize Draw... Probably every fourth name on the electoral roll. Still, in with a chance... Done by high-tech computer, I suppose. Or just low-tech luck. 'Some call it chance, and some God,' as someone once said. I wish it had been me...

O Divinity of Lotteries, isn't it my turn by *now*? Please God, let me win the big one. Preferably before the water rates are due.

Growing up to pray

When I was a child, as the man said (1 Corinthians 13:1, if you must know), I thought like a child. And I prayed like a child. But now, now that I am *so* grown up...?

In childhood I prayed first for Mummy and Daddy; for Smoky the cat and for Teddy. I was a little ashamed of praying for Teddy (although not for the cat). I prayed for them all, but I didn't pray for any particular things for them. I just sort of thought of them, and I thought of God, and said—as I'd heard others say—'Amen' at the end. 'So be it.' 'Do what you will with them.'

Of course it has been downhill all the way since then.

When a little older I prayed for things, rather than for people. Things for me (exam-things as well as bike-things) and very particular things for very particular other people. Until, with an adult's perspective and concerns, the list of things—and people—became very long. Much too long. So it all began to fall apart.

Is that what prayer is really about? Asking for the moon for everyone on the earth? Or had the child got it right? (It wouldn't be the first time.)

Praying for Thingy

Jesus told his disciples that it was OK to pray for things. His prayer, 'The Lord's Prayer', is partly a prayer for 'our daily bread' and 'deliverance from evil'. Yet it is mainly a prayer to become related to *God*: that God should forgive us, that God's will should be done, that God's holiness should be recognized, and that God's Kingdom should be established.

Religion says that there is only one thing in the end worth asking for, for ourselves and others: God. And the only thing God can give us that can be guaranteed, and that will last, is God.

'The only thing God can give us'—always, unconditionally, certainly—'is himself.'

Prayer in our need and suffering, and prayers for others in their needs and suffering, are deep religious responses to lives going wrong. In commending those lives to God we are speaking of them in the same breath as we speak of God. This is not necessarily a matter of asking for life to be different, although we can ask for that (and if prayer is to be honest, that is often what we should honestly ask for). But prayer is in the end asking that life should be in God's hands, whatever happens.

In that context, and from that perspective, religious believers can cope with suffering, failure, betrayal—even loss and death. Prayer is a matter of saying 'God' over our lives and our world, however destroyed they be. To do that is to hope... and to live again.

Prayer as relationship

Prayer is described as part of a relationship with God. As such, it must be a bit like relationships with other people. Such relationships may involve a lot of speaking, or a silent 'being in the presence' of the other. Sometimes people need to be explicit about a relationship, to 'attend' consciously to it. They do this so that it will be stronger when it slips out of their consciousness. Friendship needs to be celebrated on occasions in a special way because it is there all the time.

Prayer, it is claimed, expresses and sustains a relationship with God in the same way that what we say and do with others expresses and evokes our love for them. So the Catholic theologian Friedrich von Hügel could say: 'I do not only kiss my child because I love her, but in order to love her.' And he wasn't just talking about his daughter.

Just as relationships grow through honesty and mutual trust (being truly ourselves with our friends, without putting on our 'Sunday-best' personalities), so honesty, openness, and boldness are deemed to be essential in prayer. Similarly, as people tell their close friends things about themselves that they know already (such as 'I trust you'), so it is with a God who knows everything about everyone. This 'telling all' clearly can and should include expressions of despair and misery, bitterness and anger against God. These cries from the heart are there in many of the Psalms. Prayers may also, possibly, include a little humour:

> *Lord, you know better than I know myself that I am getting older and will some day be old. Keep me from the fatal habit of thinking I must say something on every subject and on every occasion. Release me from craving to straighten out everybody's affairs. Make me thoughtful but not moody: helpful but not bossy. With my vast store of wisdom it seems a pity not to use it all, but you know, Lord, that I want a few friends at the end.*
>
> ATTRIBUTED (BUT SURELY FALSELY!) TO A SEVENTEENTH-CENTURY NUN

What do people really want out of a relationship? True friends only want the relationship of friendship itself: 'Do not seek my money, or power, or sexual charms. If you want only them, you don't really want me. The only thing I have to give you is myself.' In prayer, some say, we learn that the only thing worth wanting is God: 'Seek first the Kingdom...'

Menus and shopping lists

The mnemonic ACTS has been used to summarize the types of Christian prayer: it stands for *A*doration, *C*onfession, *T*hanksgiving and *S*upplication.

❑ In adoration people praise God for what he is. Prayer expresses and strengthens our sense of wonder and awe, and (as a response) our love and self-offering. God is the source and focus of all that Christians value most highly and unconditionally. They claim that people only know God truly if they truly adore him. As the song has it: 'to know him is to love him'.

❑ In confession Christians acknowledge their separation from God ('sin'), through their own wrongdoing ('sins'). As they recognize and express their inadequacy before God, they come to see more clearly the extent of his accepting love. They thus learn to live with themselves in hope. Sometimes this forgiveness of God may be formally declared in an absolution.

❏ In thanksgiving God is thanked for what he does. Thankfulness can be an expression of hope and an expression of the meaningfulness of life. When you thank God for the specific, particular good things of life, you acknowledge that such things reveal most clearly the character of God. But Christians are also encouraged in the New Testament to thank God 'always for all things'. To thank God is to see life, the world and others not just as neutral objects, but as *gifts*.

❏ Supplication (either 'petitions' for oneself or 'intercessions' for others) is only a part of prayer, but it leads to most of the problems. All agree that prayer has an effect on the one who prays. But does this sort of prayer have an effect on God also? Some Christians claim that we should not think like this, for that would be to try to influence God's will, or even to perform miracles (by proxy) mechanically or magically. Others, however, see praying for things and expecting answers to prayer as essential to true religious belief. Both positions need to deal with those occasions when prayers are not 'answered'. (We recall that Paul had the same problem, but that his faith found a new depth precisely because God did *not* answer his prayer. See Chapter 19.)

The following points have been made by different Christians in reflecting on 'answers to prayer':

❏ If God is personal, no magic is involved. This sort of prayer is a request; God is not compelled to respond. (Or, if you prefer, God's 'answer' might be 'No'.)

❏ Those who seem to trust God most completely often do seem to be able to 'trust him to answer their prayers'. But these—like all true prayers—must in the end be prayers for God to be God, and to rule (God's 'Kingdom').

❏ One cannot pray for miracles that one does not believe in. Nor should people work up guilt feelings about their own 'lack of faith'. Honesty with God includes honesty not only about what we want, but also about what we expect. Perhaps the 'measure of faith' that people have may itself be God's gift, and not our own creation.

❏ Sometimes the world needs to be *changed*: to be recreated 'nearer to the heart's desire'. But sometimes it has to be *accepted* as it is: along with its evil, our broken hopes and unanswered prayers (as with Jesus in Gethsemane?). Prayer, all Christians claim, changes our perspective about ourselves, others and God. It should make us more honest before God, more concerned for others and more committed to God's will. In prayers for ourselves and others, those who pray may learn more about their true needs. And they may be able more clearly to distinguish their needs from their more superficial 'wants'. In prayer, we should become more ready to accept whatever God brings. Perhaps this is a way of becoming less 'anxious about tomorrow', which lies in God's hands (see Chapter 21).

❏ In the past, most Christians prayed for rain and miracles. Now some only pray for psychological changes—fortitude, generosity, and guidance for the doctor's skill. Is that a real difference? If God intervenes in someone's mind, is that 'easier' than intervening in nature?

❏ Can Christians consistently say that God 'cannot' perform miracles in answer to prayer, or only that he often 'does not'? Some believe that God will very often intervene in the world to answer a faithful prayer; others that he never does so (see Chapter 9). The position of most people who pray lies somewhere between these two extremes. Openness in a relationship with God may include an openness to whatever God may do (or not do) in response to prayer.

❏ Parents who give their children everything they ask for may not be teaching those children anything about trust or love in a relationship. A universe where God is for ever 'popping in' to change things diminishes the opportunity for human beings to behave responsibly themselves. If God is always going to bail you out then choice, judgment and moral decision disappear.

❏ A relationship with God *is* different from that with our closest friends. God is the Holy One, the ultimate Mystery. God is the one who is there, who hears, when there is no one there, no one to hear. God may be very close, but no person could know God inside out. Humans can only know the 'outskirts of his ways'. Religious women and men often do not know what God is about. But they may trust him all the same.

29 Security Systems...

A Dangerous Journey?

I went to Oslo once, to see Edvard Munch's painting *The Scream*. It is a deeply disturbing painting. A man stands at what looks like a long jetty. In the far distance stand other figures, detached, uninvolved. Family? Friends? Passers-by? We cannot tell. What grips the attention is the face of the figure in the foreground. It is caught in a ghastly rictus of pain, a spasm of horror. Out of its mouth comes a writhing shape, the scream of the title, a little like a cartoon speech bubble, except that the effect is anything but amusing. The scream almost seems alive; it twists and contorts; and physically *fills* the picture. It is an appalling statement of Munch's view of the world, of what it feels like to be lost, of a universe that is tearing apart, of a human being about to fall into the abyss.

That is one nightmare. Different, though related, fears are touched in the *Aliens* series of films. In this sci-fi futuristic horror groups of space explorers venture out into the unknown. In an atmosphere of mounting menace we discover that no one is ultimately safe. Though colleagues and friends intend to stand together, at any moment any one of them may be taken by alien beings and the heroine will be left alone. Abandoned by those she believed were on her side, unable to trust anyone, facing creatures which are driven by insatiable and primeval appetites, it's a wonder Sigourney Weaver isn't reduced to a gibbering heap. Every subliminal nightmare is played out for all it's worth. *Aliens* is vampires, spiders, blood-sucking leeches, killer sharks and jellyfish all on one screen at the same time. Out there is something immensely powerful, hostile, destructive, sadistic, pitiless. It hates me and will destroy me if it can. Worse still, it will feed off my innermost self, sucking out the life, while holding me suspended in limitless pain. Thus every fear and phobia is brought to the surface. At least the audience gets its money's worth.

Such films work, and presumably make money, because they draw on feelings which are primal. The child who cries inconsolably when the parent leaves the bedroom is afraid of the dark, and all the nameless horrors of a cold, impersonal, uncaring universe. But the sense that everything is falling apart and I cannot hold it together for much longer is not confined to children. It was graphically expressed by a woman who said, 'My life's like a child's cat's cradle of string. If I let one taut connection go slack then I am done for.' We may think that ideas of guilt and uncleanness are primitive; they have a way of reappearing in un-suspected places. So a rape victim may express a totally irrational feeling of pollution and defilement and may need psychotherapeutic healing of the memories or a medieval rite of purification.

Nor is the sense of being lost only to be communi-cated in the feverish colours and shapes of Edvard Munch. The American psychologist James Fowler tells a tale of a chance companion in a taxi who said,

'If we have any purpose on this earth, it is just to keep things going. We can stir the pot while we are here and try to keep things interesting. Beyond that everything runs down: your marriage runs down, your body runs down, your faith runs down. We can only try to make it interesting.'

Though this seems at first hearing remarkably acute and realistic, yet it is a kind of confession of lostness. In the end everything is pointless.

We can see more domestic examples of insecurity in the measures adopted to keep our possessions safe from the predator. Out there is a jungle. By night we lock ourselves safely in the house-fortress, pull up the draw-bridge and drop the portcullis (or at least put the chain on the door). Alas, infinitely precious things (like the car) remain outside, exposed and vulnerable. The crime prevention officer comes like a teacher of ancient wisdom to show us how to be safe. Guru-like he intones: 'Lock all doors and windows; never leave valuables in the car; never leave the key in the ignition; fit an anti-thief device, a steering-wheel lock and a car alarm; use security-coded equipment for your car stereo; put your aerial down; have your registration number etched on your windows. Best of all, put your car in the garage and never get it out.' As the Book of Common Prayer has it, 'Defend us from all perils and dangers of this night... ' All very prudent and sensible, when you are talking about cars... but what if the burglar is a cosmic burglar and the prey is my very self?

Cutting your losses
These feelings were not unknown to the writers of the Bible. Indeed, from one perspective the Bible can be seen as a book which focuses on the problem of loss: loss of joy, loss of meaning, loss of innocence, loss of security. Humankind loses a garden by an act of disobedience—and with that loss falls prey to a multitude of ills. Things fall apart. Whether the threat is loss of paradise, or death, or slavery to unseen and malevolent powers, or deportation by invading kings; whether, in a more modern idiom, it is a sense of the pointlessness of it all or a deep-seated inability to live a properly human life or a fracture in the structure of society or a sense of being alienated from any source of personal hope, yet humanity usually acknowledges that there is a problem. Systems of salvation are affirmations of faith—that what is fundamentally wrong can be set right, that there is a bedrock security somewhere, if only you know where to look for it.

151

Christianity is a salvation religion, that is, it is about being saved or rescued. Against the numberless fears referred to above, it sets the (perhaps unlikely) declaration that reality is personal, that the universe is not out of control, that what has been lost can be regained or at least transformed, that the hands of God are not those of the cosmic sadist but unconditional love. The focus of these assertions lies in the life, death and resurrection of Jesus Christ. He is the sharp end of the message, its definitive expression and the touchstone of human response.

The phrase 'human response' reminds us that salvation is not mechanical or automatic. Short of personal physical assault it is difficult to rescue someone who refuses to be rescued. Christianity has always assumed that people have the freedom to be resistant. Not every announcement of salvation has to be greeted with little whoops of joy. Perhaps the confident assertions of the preceding paragraph sound like pure fairytale and wishful fantasy to many readers. 'Well, it would be nice but reality keeps breaking in.'

For one person it may be temperamentally very difficult to believe that the universe is anything other than impersonal or uncaring. To another, traumatic experiences may have driven them to believe that everything is falling apart; that there is no meaning apart from the meaning you make up for yourself. Yet another may feel so personally polluted or guilty that he or she despairs of ever finding release or a new beginning. There doesn't seem to be a sure-fire way of adjudicating between these conflicting positions. Christian good news or religious escapism? The only way in? Or a cheap and dishonest way out? Traditionally, I suppose Christians have tried to tackle the question with a combination of responses. They have pointed to Jesus and said, 'See if you don't find him and his message coherent and attractive.' They have 'given testimony', saying something like, 'This is my story; consider whether it might be yours.' And they have prayed for divine revelation; that is, for God to open people's eyes and enable them to 'see' the truth for themselves. Beyond these three moves I'm not quite sure how it would be possible to convince someone of the truth of the Christian vision of the world over against some other picture.

What gets saved?

Whatever the truth of the matter, it won't hurt to explore the concept of salvation a little further. According to Christians, what exactly is it that gets saved? There is a caricature which restricts salvation to the soul—and thinks of it as laundering some invisible, intangible, elusive 'bit of spiritual stuff' floating around somewhere inside us. A more constructive (and orthodox) view sees salvation as multi-dimensional. The Hebrew word *shalom* catches the scope of the term. Salvation transforms human beings in all their relationships; it affects the 'soul', in the sense of people in their relationship towards God, but it also touches their social life, their family relationships, the way they view and treat creation, their attitude towards structures and institutions. Shalom is 'peace' or 'wholeness'. It includes healing of the body, restoration of broken relationships, inner contentment, justice in society, a renewed creation and peace with God. In liberation theology it might mean the end of economic injustice; in pastoral care, healing of the memories; in confession of guilt, forgiveness of sin.

The tenses of salvation

The idea of wholeness raises the issue of the right tense for salvation. People sometimes come to faith with lives which are deeply damaged; personalities and character traits don't alter overnight; structures and relationships take a long time to change. Salvation is not just about a past transformation followed by instant perfection. The word relates to past, present and future.

It may make things clearer to explore a parallel situation where salvation or 'rescue' is involved. We are unfortunately only too aware of the phenomenon of hostage taking. John McCarthy, Brian Keenan, Terry Waite and others spent long years in captivity at the hands of terrorist groups. Eventually they were released. As a result of negotiation, political pressure, protest and appeals their release was effected. People might have been tempted to say that the rescue was over and done with. And in a sense it was. They were free. But in fact the moment of rescue marked the beginning of a long process of debriefing and of learning to live again in the normal world. The hostages needed medical care and a healthy diet, they needed to be reintroduced gradually into the pace of modern life, they had to learn to relate to their families and friends. Perhaps most importantly they needed help to face the memories of their ordeal. Hurts and traumas do not disappear immediately. They are taken on into the new life. Nevertheless everyone involved with the hostages looks forward to a time when the damage suffered during captivity has been totally healed. At that point the rescue may be said to be complete.

The same three tenses recur in the Christian understanding of salvation. It is a past event. The Christian looks back to the death and resurrection of Christ. The results of those events for the individual are described in terms of 'being pronounced not guilty', 'being reconciled with God', 'being released from slavery'. The Christian is delivered from the effects of sin, from the condemnation which is linked with it and from alienation from God. But salvation is also a present process. The Spirit of God is constantly at work cleaning up the damage of the old life. The 'harvest of the Spirit' consists of a Christlike lifestyle—love, joy, peace, patience, long-suffering. However, few would claim that Christians were squeaky clean or anything like perfect. Most show their human side quickly enough, especially on a Monday morning in November. So the New Testament looks forward to a time when the project will be completed. The Bible's image of a new Jerusalem adorned like a bride points to a time when sin, fear, crying and death will be no more.

30 Hell is...

A Wasted Journey?

The experience of loss is common to all human
beings. Every child has to come to terms with it at
some point. The hamster isn't coming back, the ice-
cream has been licked into extinction, the melted
snowman has gone for good. But the idea of hell
poses the question of loss in a painfully sharp form.
How can Christians conceive of a human being
permanently losing out—being deprived of everything
that makes humanity worthwhile? And for that matter
how can Christians get their minds round the loss
experienced by God? Not everything in the garden is
lovely; in the end the family is incomplete and
destined to stay so.

One way in is to reflect on what happens when a
relationship goes dead. The dialogue below is about a
domestic tragedy. Does it parallel the cosmic tragedy
between God and humanity?

*I didn't know how it would be, at first, you know. He seemed like
everything I'd ever wanted—good-looking, kind, caring. Mister
Wonderful.*

> *When did you suspect there was something wrong?*

*I'm not sure. There were one or two moments even before we
got married. Little things. I remember he broke an ornament I
had—nothing special, just a tiny vase—but he... he threw it
across the room. Because I wouldn't go out with him one
evening. And I'd fixed something up with a friend of mine. He
was... unreasonable in that kind of way.*

> *And later?*

Oh, later... it was the pits. I ended up in the County Hospital once... with a broken jaw and a couple of cracked ribs. Almost anything could set him off. And my mum would go on and on about walking out on him. But I never did.

Why was that? No one could have blamed you.

Well, you'll think me nutty or something... but I loved him. Yes, I know, it's daft isn't it? I was a walking casualty department and I stuck it out. Even now I miss him. And I know he was a real sod but... can't explain it.

Did he love you?

Well, I think he did at the beginning. But... I'm not kidding myself. I think this is what hurts so much. There was a moment when he just went dead. I can remember him kicking me... I was hanging on to the kitchen table... I thought he'd kill me... and he was screaming 'I hate you, you little bitch.' And I realized he meant it. Funny thing, because he'd probably said worse to me before. But I knew he meant it this time. And something had died in him. There was no getting him back then. Just a matter of time before he went off with her.

How did you feel then?

How was I supposed to feel? Just working out time... treading water. It was all finished. There was nothing in him that I could touch anymore. And nothing much in me... except this feeling that I'd lost him for good and all... and I wasn't ever going to get him back.

It's hell to understand

Another way to approach the concept of hell is through pictures. Of course we need to be sensible about this. The world of eternity is inconceivable. Our pictures of it are not to be taken literally, otherwise we shall end up again with devils in red tights with toasting forks. The paintings of the medieval artist Hieronymus Bosch are vivid enough, but tell us more about his nightmares than the temperature of hell. On the other hand, pictures are not useless. We can take them seriously even if we cannot say exactly what it is they point towards.

If this is so then the New Testament offers us a range of images. Hell is 'a darkness outside' and 'a lake of fire'. There is 'wailing and gnashing of teeth'; 'the worm dieth not'. It is like being on the wrong side of a locked door, while the banquet goes on merrily inside; like being on the far side of a vast chasm. The Greek word for hell is *Gehenna*, a reference to the valley of the Hinnom on the south side of Jerusalem. This was the city rubbish dump where the fires burned continuously, and everything was destroyed.

What is the best way to make sense of all these pictures? One common move is to stress the *freedom* of human beings. The argument runs something like this. The perfect love of God cannot force people into a free response of acceptance. If it did so then freedom would not be freedom and love would be coercive—hardly what one expects of love. The whole transaction would end up as its opposite. What's a kiss worth if it is the result of blackmail or taken by force? But if humans are free to accept God's advances then they must be equally free to reject them. This decision, though deeply distressing to God, is one which he must respect. Hell has been called the greatest compliment that God can pay to humans, because it shows that he takes their choices seriously. Someone who refuses to breathe will die, even though the air around him exerts its gentle and insistent pressure.

Another move is to emphasize the enormity of wrongdoing. Some sins so totally offend our conception of what it is to be human that they seem to cry out for a curse or punishment of supernatural proportions. What kind of a universe do we live in if at the end of time monstrous acts of cruelty are just passed over? It is not enough to say that God will judge them if by that we just mean that he will say that they were wrong, even if his judgment is the last word on the subject? How would we react to a judge who did nothing more than wring his hands over the rapist or the drunk driver who has just killed four children and say, 'I disapprove. I disapprove'? If the world is founded on justice then somewhere, somehow, sometime, justice must be vindicated. Something has got to be done and not just said.

A third line of argument makes the obvious point that heaven and hell are not places. They are ways of talking about a *state or*

157

condition. What God offers is a relationship with himself. The image is one of seeing someone face to face. But what may be unutterably fantastic for one person, the ultimate vision of beauty, may be indescribably awful to another. It all depends on your attitude. Hell now describes the situation of someone, who along with the rest of mankind, enters the presence of God and gazes on God's face. For this person the experience is terrible. To feel those eyes boring into you and not to be able to escape them becomes a kind of torment. But the 'fault' would not be in God. He is the same to everyone. It's like going to a party and hating every minute of it.

A fourth way into the idea of hell stresses the *inevitability* of it all. It is not that God is punitive and spiteful. He is certainly not the cosmic sadist of some people's imagination. The fault, according to this view, lies in our inadequate understanding of the nature of sin. Try seeing sin as a kind of virus in the cosmic computer. It is not possible for the virus and the program to co-exist. A virus that was so malign as to unformat the disks or attack the deep structure of the computer would mean the end of the computer as we know it. In reality the situation is rather more grave than this. We are not referring to computers but to the divine will, that principle which ensures that anything exists at all. When sin and holiness meet, the universe isn't big enough to hold them both.

Hell to believe

Someone may object that God has done a pretty good job of putting up with sin for the last several thousand years. Why does everything have to be so final? After all, if God is limitlessly knowledgeable, everlastingly patient and eternally loving, then surely he will know how to break down the defences of even the most resistant person—eventually. Everlasting love, if you take the word 'everlasting' seriously, will find a way in the end. A therapist with limitless patience and infinite skill would be able to get through to even the most withdrawn and traumatized child.

This is an attractive view and has led some Christians to *universalism*—the idea that everyone will be won over in the end. It is usually an expression of hope that God's forgiveness and patience are both unending.

However, its defect may lie in too easy an assumption that our decisions leave us unaffected. It is a different matter if each little rejection of God and goodness deadens, however slightly, our capacity to respond. Then the picture of the life-support machine may be nearer the mark. While there is some possibility of recovery the machine is left on. But sometimes the point is reached when the patient no longer possesses any capacity for personal, unassisted living. The only course left open to the grieving relatives is to pull the plug. A mirror may become so crazed that it is worthless as a mirror. So the image of God in humanity may be so marred that it is incapable of reflecting his life. But this story-metaphor suggests that hell is just another word for 'extinction'.

Perhaps we are too curious about hell. The New Testament reminds us that the judgment is God's, not ours. What can be said with fair certainty is that there will be many surprises. The Gospels bristle with paradoxes. 'The first will be last and the last first'; 'the righteous', who served Christ unwittingly, are amazed at his acceptance of them; those who cry 'Lord, Lord' but for whom it is all words, are rejected; the rich man goes to hell, the poor beggar to Abraham's bosom; the tax-collectors and prostitutes press into God's Kingdom before the righteous and religious Pharisees.

'Let him who thinks he stands take heed lest he fall.' There's not a lot to be smug about.

> We should be able to speak of Hell only with tears.
>
> John Stott

31 The Nine O'Clock News...

A Dead-End Journey?

A man dies. God knows, it happens often enough. Shot to pieces, blown to bits, starving by inches, mangled on the motorway or just made to 'disappear' by some South American secret police force. We catch thirty seconds of it on the car radio and switch channels. It's a pity, of course, but there's such a lot of it about. Compassion deficit sets in.

Occasionally a death becomes larger than the simple fact. The murder of James Bulger felt like a glimpse into hell. The Buerk Report on Ethiopia was concentrated into one image—the starving child trying to stand up. The deaths of Steve Biko and Jan Palach in their time were symbols and calls to a struggle for life. The deaths of President Kennedy and Martin Luther King provoked earthquakes within the nation.

And the death of Jesus possesses an extraordinary resilience. Dislodged from consciousness his cross re-enters everywhere, in Scorcese's film, *The Last Temptation of Christ*, in a Requiem Mass or Lloyd Webber's *Jesus Christ Superstar*, in the sign made by an athlete before the Olympic 100-metres final, in wayside calvaries in the South of France, parodied in *The Life of Brian*, painted by Raphael and Salvador Dali or etched into a hot cross bun. It seems to be one of those deaths that are bigger than the facts.

Dying crimson
The facts themselves are relatively straightforward.

The career of a promising if controversial young Jewish preacher came to a sorry end. Apparently determined to force the issue, Jesus travelled south to Jerusalem and entered the city if not in a blaze of glory, at least with enough noise to alert the authorities. At the Jewish festival of Passover, of all times, it was essential to keep the place incident-free. Both Herod and Pilate felt that the the situation was volatile enough to bring them from the luxury of Caesarea and Herodium into the powder keg of Jerusalem. Passover was always likely to be a time when fanatics attempted to turn their Messianic fantasies of saving the nation from Roman rule into reality. Just keep the place under tight control for a week, double up the military presence but avoid provoking the loony left. With luck we might all get back to the summer palaces with our reputations intact.

But as everyone knows, this Passover began in the worst possible way—with a triple crucifixion.

Jesus was nailed to the cross, the most painful method of crucifixion, itself the most barbarous of punishments. During the period of hanging on the cross he was taunted by onlookers but watched by a tiny group of faithful followers. The Gospels record seven 'words' from him, including a startling and horrifying cry of abandonment, 'My God, my God, why have you forsaken me?' He was dead in a relatively short time and because of this his legs remained unbroken. Towards late afternoon his body was taken down to avoid polluting the Sabbath.

But this complex of events has evoked more response than any other event in history. It is impossible to exaggerate the effect of those few hours on the history of the world. In itself the event was straightforward enough. It was not the first or last time that a trouble-maker has been executed by an occupying power. What has engaged the imagination of the world is the meaning of the event. Somewhere in there, thousands have felt, is the key to understanding the riddle of our existence. At one level you can supply a political interpretation of the death. But this is strangely unsatisfying. Why did Jesus die? And why is this death celebrated by Christians every year at Easter and every day in the Eucharist, in sermon, prayer and hymn, in stained glass, painting and sculpture? Why is it felt to be of personal significance? The words of Isaac Watts are echoed by literally millions of Christians:

His dying crimson like a robe
Spreads o'er his body on the tree.
And I am dead to all the world
And all the world is dead to me.

Cross-words or touch wood

The church has wrestled for centuries with the meaning of the crucifixion. Sometimes it has been presented as the ultimate visual aid. It is the manifestation in time of something that God in eternity has always and will always feel. It embodies God's love in a way that nothing else can. Just as cutting across a tree trunk will reveal, literally in a cross-section, the rings which run all the way through the trunk, so this death is a cross-section of what is eternally true. God loves humanity... everlastingly, unconditionally, with no escape clause and far beyond the point of no return.

A second interpretation fastens on the cross as a victory and Christ as a conqueror. The line in *Jesus Christ Superstar*—'to conquer death you only have to die'—gives us the clue. God comes in the person of Christ (see Chapter 38) and takes all that evil can throw at him, to the extent of dying. But the quality of his dying—innocent, obedient, and without bitterness—turns what might seem like defeat into victory. Easter Day shows that for the person who 'locks onto' Christ, death becomes 'the gate of life immortal'; the believer walks behind Christ along a path which he has already opened up.

Yet a third interpretation emphasizes the perfect holiness of God and the fact that it is not possible for imperfect, sinful humanity to approach him. The problem, in a sense, lies within God's own being. On this view the crucifixion is where God-in-Christ experiences the full separation from God which is the inevitable effect of human sin. The wrath of God burns itself out in Christ who is a kind of substitute for humanity. His cry of desolation from the cross—'My God, why have you abandoned me?'—points towards this interpretation. This view has the great merit of taking human sin and divine holiness seriously. Though it is easy to caricature as divine sadism, it does at least do justice to the cross as a place where something was done on humanity's behalf which we could not do for ourselves.

A final explanation makes much of the connection between Christ's death and the life which preceded it. Christ is a new kind of humanity, a sort of Adam-Mark-Two (see Chapter 8). His life follows exactly the pattern which God intended for us and culminates in a death which is the fitting climax to a life of perfect obedience. Christ is thus our *representative* rather than our substitute. He is what we ought to be. Those who are 'in Christ' enjoy all the blessings of his new humanity—life, peace, power and reconciliation with God.

These traditional explanations, laboriously constructed from metaphors and images, may seem too verbose to strike fire. The church has never issued an approved version of the doctrine of the *atonement*—that is, the way in which God reconciles rebellious and alienated humanity to himself. The cross of Christ remains a mystery. Christians are always guilty of talking too much.

Nevertheless, the feeling remains... a man dies. God knows, it happens often enough. But this death, in some haunting way, might be of personal significance to me.

In his dying might be hidden the secret of my living.

SECTION 5

Who Are We?

The older you get, the more you realize that the really simple questions, like 'Who am I?', 'What's the meaning of life?' and 'Where did I put my keys?' are the really difficult ones to answer. What is it about people that's really important, that makes us all human—even the really annoying ones, you know who I mean...?

32 Car, Bus or Tram...

Choosing People?

> *There once was a man who said, 'Damn!*
> *It appears to me now that I am*
> > *An engine that moves*
> > *In determinate grooves,*
> *Not a taxi or bus, but a tram.'*
> ANON

In David Lodge's novel *Small World*, Robin Dempsey
gets so very depressed that he turns for comfort to a
computer. He knows that this computer runs the ELIZA
program, which simulates the conversation of a good
counsellor. (Interestingly enough, such a program does
actually exist in real life, and not just in the novel!)
Every time he types in, 'I'm not feeling any better' or
'Nobody seems to like me', it displays on its screen the

messages: 'Tell me about it' or 'What makes you say that?' The sessions go on for hours. Josh Collins, a computer programmer, looks on and is highly amused.

The story tells us something about counselling and something about people. Both men know that Robin was 'talking' to a machine, programmed to respond to a particular input with a particular output. But one of them thought that it was a great joke that anyone would treat this as a serious conversation. The other didn't.

What if we turn the story into science fiction? The computer is now very high-tech, and hidden in a totally convincing simulated human form: an android. You meet it ('her', 'him'?) at a party; talk, share confidences; meet several times; fall in love. The day before the wedding you get a telephone call. 'Hi, I'm your friend's programmer. Just what do you want it (her, him) to do next?'

You stand in the church or register office next to your beloved android. If you are a chauvinistic male it would now be programmed, perhaps, to be submissive and get on with the housework without complaining—as in the film *The Stepford Wives*. More generally, imagine that it is programmed to behave in whatever way you think your perfect mate should behave.

Is that situation just the same as any human-human marriage? It may well be a less fraught marriage, and a less risky relationship; but the deeper question is: is it a *real* human relationship?

What is the difference between human beings and machines, especially complex, sophisticated computers? The element that seems to be missing is freedom. The android's behaviour is predetermined: if the program and the input together tell it to jump, it jumps. Human spouses are different. Many people would say that a human being is not free unless he or she *could* have acted otherwise. We may have given in to the strongest impulse when we stay in bed all day or punch the boss on the nose. 'But you must realize,' people say, 'that you were free to do otherwise.'

Were we? Are we?

Any old excuse?

People sometimes deny this, particularly in court. 'I couldn't help myself, your honour.' Standing before the judgment seat of God we might also be tempted to say, 'Just a minute, what about my genes and environment and those other extenuating circumstances, your honour... er, your infinite holiness?'

And, of course, we would have a point. Religious people sometimes talk as if human freedom is unlimited: determined by nothing outside our own will. God, presumably, should know better. God knows how restricted our choices and behaviour really are. In fact *only* God could know that.

The world may praise some people as saints whose nature, upbringing, emotional life and situation mean that they hardly have to exert any 'free will' to do what is right. But perhaps the *real* saints are less visible. They are people who often succumb to the temptation to sin, but are nevertheless trying hard to resist it. They are exerting their freedom, but against very high odds.

'Judgment is mine, says the Lord.' And a good job too. Only God could know where real freedom and responsibility really lie.

But this can be no excuse *for ourselves*. I cannot say: I'm a tram, so don't blame me. I'm a tram, except when I do something right (and then I'm a very good little bus). Nor can we say to our husbands, wives, colleagues or friends, 'I cannot help it, I had to do it—and do it (breaking into song) my way'—and *then* get angry if *they* go off and have an affair, steal the petty cash or drop us in it. That would be neither rational nor fair.

At the end of John Braine's novel *Room at the Top*, Joe Lampton—the original 'angry young man'—is overcome by guilt because he has jilted Alice in favour of the wealthy Susan, and Alice has driven her car into a wall. He will not be comforted:

*'Oh, God,' I said, 'I did kill her. I wasn't there, but I killed
her.'*

*Eva drew my head on to her breast. 'Poor darling, you
mustn't take on so. You don't see it now, but it was all for
the best. She'd have ruined your whole life. Nobody blames
you, love. Nobody blames you.'*

*I pulled myself away from her abruptly. 'Oh my God,' I
said, 'that's the trouble.'*

JOHN BRAINE

Taking me seriously

We may not be completely free, but we don't view our actions and
choices as being completely determined by factors outside our
control. Somehow, in order to be fully human, we have to
acknowledge our responsibility—and our freedom. We don't
really think that *we* are androids. If we did, we should take
ourselves less seriously.

And most religious believers claim that God would also. Why
should God bother with this creation at all if he wanted us to
have no say in the way it runs? He might as well have created a
race of Nintendo machines to play with. Yet God must know that
if you give people freedom you run a great risk. Give people
freedom, and there's a real chance they will tell you where to
stick your commandments.

But if you *don't* give them freedom, you don't make them into
people. It might be nice when the good-looking android gives you
a cuddle. But it's not really her/his/its choice, not her/his/its
decision. It isn't a free response. So it's not worth much.

Only free responses *count*.

Divine dilemma

God's dilemma, then, is that he can create *either* a perfect and
obedient race without freedom, *or* he can create this lot. A tough
choice to make.

In his book *The Worlds of Science and Religion*, the philosopher of religion Don Cupitt offers us two parables to aid this
discussion.

In the first a film director has been shooting a film, rewriting
and recasting as he goes along, and is left with a large stock of

'rushes' from which he assembles several different versions of the film. He now has to choose one for release. He runs them all through and chooses the best. Cupitt writes: 'Within the chosen version the personae must act plausibly and stay "in character". It makes no sense to ask that the heroine at some point behave differently, for that would be to ask for one of the suppressed versions, and the director has already chosen the best.'

Cupitt's other parable describes a novelist who begins with a setting, a range of characters, and a theme, but 'lets the plot work itself out in the writing, as he goes along'. The novelist is able to let his characters loose on the page, 'to let *them* determine the details of the plot as he writes'. Everything remains under the novelist's control, the theme is his, and he is going to ensure that it ends properly, 'but within that overall framework he is content to let the characters work out their own destinies'.

These are, of course, parables of two ways that believers may think of God's relationship to the world. In the first, God's omnipotence and omniscience are shown in God's determining beforehand 'every detail of the world-process'. In the second, his power and wisdom are revealed in a very different way, in the 'self-restraint by which he is able to allow the world-process to unfold itself', while retaining the power to guide it towards the conclusion he intends.

The second picture gives a better account of human freedom. It perhaps also gives a better account of the status God must give to us.

33 Images...

Reflective People?

Changing your image can be a pricey business. It may involve a new colour-coded wardrobe, a personal hairstylist, a change of car and possibly of psychotherapist... it all mounts up. There are cheaper ways, of course. Who knows what's going on inside the head of the middle-aged man with a paunch who jogs past you in the early morning darkness? Day-dreams cost nothing.

Perhaps I'll have a little rest by the next letterbox. Mustn't overdo it. I think it's running with my Walkman playing **Chariots of Fire** that's the problem. The pace is a bit quick. But as Coleman said, 'This is absolutely amazing... Linford Higgins has opened up a gap of two hundred metres! It's a phenomenal performance!'

Just a little breather... Jogging's not everything. Here I can muse and reflect on the human condition in between gasps. The Bertrand Russell of Peabody Gardens, they will call me. 'Few contemporary philosophers have so economically, yet elegantly, explored the interstices of mind and cosmos as Ludwig Higgins in his later work...' Or perhaps poetry... I may decline the post of Poet Laureate. It's so demeaning having to write to order. I need to be touched by the Muse; then let the fire fall... 'Have you read the latest Dylan Higgins, **Under Milk Maid?**—It's really good.'

Ten past... Time to get back and have a shower. From which I shall slip, glowing, sensuous, irresistibly attractive to women... every muscle rippling as I let the bathrobe fall from my sculptured shoulders... 'Every woman was aware of Arnold Schwartzenhiggins, the 100 per cent testosterone container.'

Looks like rain. I shall drive to work... expertly, incisively... Damon Higgins in pole position. And tonight... I, Casanova Higgins, will touch the stars... and make the earth move...

The idea of an image is a common one in ordinary life. The ten-pence piece carries the image of the Queen; we say of a baby, 'He's the spitting image of his grandad'; professional photographers speak about 'images' rather than snapshots. In each case something or someone 'carries' the likeness of something else. So when God makes humanity, male and female, in the Old Testament book of Genesis, he stamps them with his image. People are made in God's likeness.

A dead-ringer for God

It is interesting to ask in what way men and women are like God. Some have said it's because they can do God-like things—they are free, they can create (although in a less impressive way), they can reason things out. Others find this a rather dry way of putting it. Human beings are called to carry God's image around by the way they live. They are meant to be little models of God, themselves little gods, the spitting image of God.

We can see this idea very clearly in the Old Testament picture of the king. Kings are the sharp end of God's rule on earth, they are the 'Lord's anointed', even the 'sons of God'. They can be described in language usually reserved for God. You do not expect a king to be 'like the rain falling on a mown field, like showers watering the earth' (Psalm 72:6) or 'the source of our life', 'God's signet-ring'. This is image language in a big way. In fact, the king is Adam before the Fall. Kings give out titles; Adam names the animals. The king is lord over his realm; Adam has dominion over the earth.

But the fact is recognized that what is true of kings is true of all people. 'What is man?' asks the Psalmist. And the answer is that we are a kind of royalty. God has made us 'a little lower than the angels', has 'crowned' us with those very royal qualities, 'glory and honour'. Men and women are sons of Adam and daughters of Eve and designed to behave like kings and queens because God has stamped them with his own sovereign image.

But if human beings are called to be living images or icons of God then this has implications for the way they behave. 'What does the Lord require?' asks the prophet Micah. 'To do justly,

love mercy and walk humbly with your God.' It is not bearing
God's image to act as if there were no tomorrow, arrogantly
domineering over those who are weaker than you, raping the
earth, destroying the animal kingdom, living more like a petty
tyrant than a just and beneficent sovereign.

Just imagine

So the image that we choose to bear is extremely important.
Human beings can bear the icon of a Hitler or an Attila the Hun.
They can model themselves on James Bond, Paul Getty, Goneril
or Lady Macbeth. But the image of the Creator remains stamped
on them. There is a kind of blueprint which depicts the way they
were created to behave.

We can see this from the other end. Every human being is
made in God's image. Therefore we are each of infinite worth. Our
value is indelibly etched into us; it is not a matter of being learned,
wealthy, intelligent, powerful, good-looking or useful to society.
Mother Teresa's work in Calcutta is done for people who are likely
to die within a few months. They are of no economic benefit to the
country, they contribute nothing to the Gross National Product.
From one point of view she is wasting both time and energy. But,
from the image-of-God perspective her efforts are not futile since
each person cared for is infinitely precious.

Sometimes these two views clash violently, as they did in the
controversy between Hitler and Dietrich Bonhoeffer, the
theologian. Bonhoeffer was chairman of the management
committee of a home for people with learning difficulties. Hitler
wished to close the home and subject the occupants to
euthanasia. Bonhoeffer, from his Christian perspective, resisted
this killing. In God's eyes, he argued, everyone was intrinsically
valuable. He saw the essential difference between his view and
that of Hitler's and knew that he had to make the protest.

There's a story about the scholar Muretus who lived in the
sixteenth century. In 1554 he became seriously ill and needed to
undergo major surgery. His chances of survival were slight. He
overheard his surgeons discussing the case. They were keen to
cut him open, not so much to effect a cure as to see what would
happen. It was close to being speculative vivisection. Speaking in
Latin, one said to the other, 'Let us experiment upon this

worthless body.' Muretus understood what was said, and painfully raising himself challenged the surgeon with these words, 'Do you call that soul worthless for whom Christ was not ashamed to die?'

This viewpoint contrasts sharply with other fashionable dogmas. Desmond Morris, the ethologist, has depicted humanity as naked apes living in a 'human zoo'. There is much truth in this, as we acknowledge elsewhere (see Chapter 35). But it is not the whole story. Neither are people rats in a Skinnerian cage, pressing levers in order to get food pellets; nor Pavlovian dogs, salivating at the sound of a bell. It is interesting that the behaviourist B.F. Skinner called one of his books *Beyond Freedom and Dignity*. Exactly.

The concept of the image of God needs to be set against views which demean humanity, however subtly expressed. It gives people worth, dignity and value. No other view has such power to awaken compassion and call forth resistance to injustice. Gerard Manley Hopkins put the point precisely:

I am all at once what Christ is, since he was what I am, and This jack, joke, poor potsherd, patch, matchwood, immortal diamond,
Is immortal diamond.

GERARD MANLEY HOPKINS

34 Inside Story...

Soulful People?

How well do we think that we know other people?
A little humility would go a long way in this area.
Especially when these other people are being selected
for some task or life's work...

*Well, ladies and gentlemen, I think we should take the
opportunity of discussing each candidate immediately after
their interview. So, then... that was Mr... Kavanagh. Would
you like to begin, George?*

*Yes, thank you, Mr Chairman. Frankly, I didn't take to him. I've
nothing against accents of course, but that grated rather on
the ear. And did you notice how he leaned forward in the
interview? A sure sign of over-defensiveness. And in my view
the tie shows a certain lack of regard for our sort of values.
He also seemed almost proud that his father was a manual
worker, when I quizzed him about his people.*

Mmm, indeed. Marion?

*Well, I have to say I was rather impressed. Penetrating eyes,
nice clear skin—you can always tell with skin, it's a window
into the personality. I see what you mean about the voice
and posture, but there's surely...*

Come on now, Marion, I'm sorry but...

Through the chair, Arthur? Thanks

*No, we have to discount the eyes in the light of the nose. And that
nose was almost illuminated! I've been around a good few
years now, and I think I'm a good judge of a man. And,
begging your pardon Marion, of a woman too... [snort]... Yes,
that's a drunk's nose. Secret drinker. Not the sort we want.*

*Point taken. Now, Mr Borrowsuck... Boiledsweet? Did you want
to say something?*

It's Borrowsweet. Er, only that he seemed to have some good ideas about worker relations, and he spoke quite convincingly on market opportunities in Eastern Europe. And his application shows that he's got two degrees—one in engineering and the other in management studies—and twenty years' experience, and one of his references did write of his 'incisive intellect', 'great integrity' and 'consistently good relationships with colleagues'.

Yes. Well, thank you for your comments, Mr Boilersuit. Very helpful, I'm sure. Nevertheless we mustn't be taken in by appearances. It's easy when you're a little inexperienced to be tempted to rather superficial judgments. There's a lot of interviewing experience around this table. No. The man's a wrong 'un. Eyes too close together, anyway. You can always tell...

More room inside?

The novelist Franz Kafka has written a witty but frightening short story called 'Metamorphosis', which begins with the startling sentence:

As Gregor Samsa awoke one morning from uneasy dreams he found himself transformed into a gigantic insect.

Gregor's dilemma is then examined in detail, as he lies on his back waving his antennae and wondering how he is going to get to work. It is bizarre, but somehow *conceivable*. Gregor has a rather different body, but he is still *really* Gregor, at least for the moment. He has the same thoughts, hopes and fears, if rather too many legs.

John Locke, the seventeenth-century English philosopher, told a similar—if *slightly* less bizarre—tale, in his story of the cobbler and the prince. Imagine the situation, he suggested, in which 'the soul of a prince, carrying with it the consciousness of the prince's past life' might 'enter and inform the body of the cobbler'. Here is republicanism-at-a-stroke, in which a member of the royal family discovers what it is like to live in the (bodily) context of his subjects, and shoe-repairers get a chance to try their hand at royal tours of the Caribbean.

Behaviourists believe that mind is an illusion and that people are to be understood simply in terms of their outer behaviour:

Two behaviourists meet in the street. One says to the other, 'You're fine, how am I?'

Locke comments that the new *prince-cobbler*, who has the cobbler's memories but the prince's body, will be recognized at court as the prince. No one there will expect him to mend their shoes. But what of the *cobbler-prince*, who has—please do try and pay attention—the cobbler's body but the prince's mind? Well everyone should recognize that he would be 'the same *person* as the prince... but he would be the same cobbler to everyone beside himself'.

Some may regard this as a rather doubtful philosophical analysis (and others as a load of old princes), but it captures a dilemma that is at the heart of any consideration of who we are.

Soulfulness

What is it about me that persists, that makes me the same person as that baby on the rug in the family snapbook? Can it be my body? But our bodies change: in the case of some of us they change grossly. At any rate there are very few cells, and comparatively few molecules, in my body now that are the same as the ones I had when I was nine months old.

Of course my present body is *continuous* with that body. If you had attached a camcorder or movie-camera to me at birth you would have one continuous (and mostly very boring) film image of my body. Fast forward and my body would be seen to change rather a lot, but it would be just as obvious that it is the same body that is changing.

What makes me the same me, then? Is it that I have the 'same body', that is that my body continues through time? The stories of Kafka and Locke suggest another answer. I am the same me, they suggest, because I am the same I: the same 'self' or 'ego', the same centre of consciousness, thought, understanding and memory. 'I am what I am,' insists Popeye, and so does each one of us. And I *know* who I am because I remember being Gregor (or whoever) yesterday, and having his memories of the day before, and so on. But am I what I am *because* there is a mysterious, elusive personal self 'inside' me? A self that *has*, not *is*, a body? A self that—at least often—remembers being the same self yesterday and last week and (sometimes) forty years ago, despite the changes in that person's body?

This is close to what many different religions and philosophies have called *the soul*; it is the domain of our subjectivity, our focal point of consciousness and activity. And it seems to be *truly* us. Lose an arm or a leg and you will be diminished as a person, but you will still be you. Lose some of your memories, or some aspects of your character and personality, and you will be changed more. Yet something seems to remain: the you that suffers this change, and experiences it.

But...
Of course these arguments are not conclusive. The brain is certainly a part of the body, but brain damage seems to be able to extinguish—or at least to affect—the mind, and perhaps the self or soul as well. Hence some philosophers severely criticize any *dualism* that distinguishes body and soul completely. But let's stay with it a little longer...

The divine spark?
Religion has often been presented as having two related concerns—God and the human soul. God is seen as like the soul: mysterious, supernatural, elusive, *spiritual* (that is, not material—made up of mind, not matter). Two thousand years ago the Roman poet Ovid wrote, 'There is a god within each human heart.' Some forms of mystical experience are thought of as directly linking God and the soul; and God is sometimes said directly to create a person's soul at birth, and to re-create—or keep in being—that soul after the death of his or her body. Hence the soul, which is said to be that part of us that is truly us and most essentially us, is God's special concern. It is in his hands, and closest to his heart.

Is all this metaphysics gone mad, or an essential truth about our humanity?

We do seem to have some sort of idea of an essential heart or core of a person. In some way it is 'inside' him or her, not on the surface. It can be 'masked' or 'hidden'. We sometimes need to 'penetrate' to it. Some people, we say, are superficial—all on the surface. They have no depth, no soul, no *inside*. Jesus, the Gospel writers tell us, did not judge people externally, but knew what was *in them*.

Inside story

This outside/inside imagery is very common in our language about people. And it fits with what we seem to find when we look 'inside' ourselves. Never without a body (or almost never—stories about 'out of body experiences' have become very popular lately), we often seem to feel that we are more than our bodies, and that that 'more' is somehow beneath and within the body. So we talk of *our* 'inner life', 'the depths' of our soul, and sometimes of the religious 'journey inwards'. If we try to say who we really are, most of us are forced back to some such 'inside story', of the I behind the eyes.

Whatever it is, whatever we are, religious believers hope that God knows it—and cares for it. After all, if it is worth preserving only God would seem to have the appropriate technology...

35 The Body in Question...

Mucky People?

The Christian doctrine of creation, properly understood, rejects the view that matter, the body and sex
are evil. It is a celebration of muck and matter, of the
body and the world, which Christianity inherited from
the Old Testament. After all, in the Book of Genesis it is
the one good God who is responsible for the existence
of matter and this God 'saw all that he had made, and
it was very good'.

This is a perspective that Judaism on the whole has
retained, while Christianity all too often has tried to
forget it, coughing in embarrassment.

One reason for this is that Christianity was
influenced early on in its history by rather alien
accounts of reality that celebrated *only* the spirit, or
the mind, or the eternal forms of things. Such views

tended to disparage the earth, the body, animals and sex—in a word, *life*.

Similar attitudes are around today, and they have their political and social consequences. Many see industry as a grubby business; and manual work as work for menials. 'Let us seek the things that are above,' some say, thinking of armchair reflection perhaps, or—if they are not up to that—commodity stockbroking.

The celebration of muck and matter

True religion, however, like true science and true life, gets its hands dirty. It both gets down to work *and*, in a way that Jesus would not have criticized, considers the lilies of the field and the birds of the air. It rejoices in them and learns from them. How could anyone really think that our humanity is *improved* by our ignorance of and separation from the rest of creation? (See also Chapter 1.)

Will the real you please stand up?

We are not *just* souls or spirits: disembodied egos with a mental life that can ignore our bodies. In this world at least, we are *embodied* selves. We may be more than our bodies, but we are at least that. Fleshed-out minds; soulful flesh. Here and now we are recognized by our bodies. ('That's Jeff, the bearded, short-sighted one. David is the other guy—the tall, athletic one with the cautious eyes.') We act through our bodies, we experience the world and other people through our bodies. In these ways we are ourselves a part of nature: DNA and protein, muck and matter. And God, Christianity claims, created and intended us to be like this. We are not angels who have got stuck in the mud by accident. This is how we *should* be.

This is the insight behind the doctrine of 'the resurrection of the body': meaning here 'the re-creation of the whole person'—material body and mind/soul together. Whatever we shall be in the future, it seems to be saying, we shall be really us. Thomas Aquinas, a great thirteenth-century theologian, argued that 'the soul has an essential and natural tendency to embodiment'.

181

Although he believed that the soul could survive the death of the body, he did not believe that my soul on its own could be really or fully me. It needs some sort of body in order to be the soul of a *person*. 'If my body is not raised,' he wrote, 'I am not raised.' A disembodied soul would be 'incomplete'—'a part out of its whole'. 'Human completion requires the resurrection of the body.'

Most Christians claim, therefore, that we shall have a new body in a new world. Some understand 'heaven' as another universe—an alternative space-time continuum. This new body will be a transformed, exalted, *different* body: a 'resurrection body'. But it will still be a material, physical body, although the laws of physics in its new universe may be different.

Ignoring the details, however, the essential claim is that we shall be embodied again: not *just* a mind, not just spirit, but the whole me.

Following the glutton?
The Christian's belief in the resurrection of Jesus, whatever the intellectual problems it raises, underlines this view of the importance and propriety of the human body. Jesus was no ascetic, subordinating his body under an extreme discipline of fasting in order to make himself holy. On the contrary he seems to have enjoyed food and wine. He showed God's compassion and acceptance to the outcasts of society and religion by partying with them, so much so indeed that his enemies could taunt: 'Look at him! A glutton and a drinker.'

Even his host at one meal was shocked when he allowed a prostitute to anoint his feet with oil of myrrh, having first washed them with her tears, kissed them and dried them with her hair. More puritanical Christians down the ages have tended to side with the Pharisee at whose table this scene took place, in thinking that Jesus should not have allowed himself to be so touched. Their concern has been not just because of 'who this woman is who is touching him', but because of the touching itself.

But Jesus is no enemy of the body, and therefore Christianity is not allowed to be. We shall see later that this is a truth that extends beyond the doctrine of resurrection to embrace Christian views on sex (Chapter 45).

Back to the animals?

But there is something more to be learned from this emphasis on our embodiment. The dignity of being called to be God's trustees, to receive God's revelation and bear God's image—indeed, to be his co-workers—isn't contradicted by our more earthy origins. Yes, we are more than the animals (see Chapter 33). But we are at least that.

And what is so wrong about being an animal? The philosopher Mary Midgley reminds us that it is we humans who kill without being hungry, and inflict physical pain and mental suffering on those who are no threat to our own survival. This is *human* behaviour, but we call it behaving *like an animal*: being 'brutal', 'bestial', 'beastly'. It's a good job that they can't understand everything that we say about them. By trying to distinguish ourselves from the beasts, Midgley says, humans have been 'mapped by reference to a landmark that is largely mythical'. Desmond Morris *has* done us a service in his popular and revealing TV programmes and books, by showing that we have a human nature that is continuous with, and builds on, our animal nature.

To recognize our kinship with other animals is to see ourselves in them, and them in us. In Midgley's words, 'Our dignity arises *within* nature, not against it.' Why are we as we are? It is partly because of evolution, from and through these other beasts. Our feelings and instincts, our bodies and behaviour, have evolved for our survival and reproduction. That does not mean that we are nothing more than a complex of animal instincts, but we *are* that and we should acknowledge it. The sexual drive that causes us so much trouble, and the

---

An American zoologist was trying to teach chimpanzees a language. He developed a complex signing system and one day signed the message that dinner was on the table when it wasn't. The chimps did not know what to do, what to make of it, what to make of him. The zoologist confessed how terrible he felt afterwards, because they hadn't yet learned how to use language to lie.

---

maternal instinct that is one of the most powerful elements of human nature, are but two features that we will understand better—and perhaps use more sensibly—if and when we take seriously their biological origin and purpose.

We need not feel ashamed to be animals, or to feel a kinship with animals. As we study them we shall learn more about ourselves, and more about God, who has created us to be like this. Such a study should certainly encourage religion to show a greater concern for ecology, for the environment that we share with the rest of creation.

Your Enjoyment of the World is never right, till you so esteem it, that everything in it, is more your treasure, then a King's exchequer full of Gold and Silver... Can you take too much joy in your Father's works? He is Himself in everything. Some things are little on the outside, and rough and common, but I remember the time, when the dust of the streets were as precious as gold to my infant eyes, and now they are more precious to the eye of reason.

You never Enjoy the World aright, till the Sea itself floweth in your veins, till you are clothed with the heavens, and crowned with the stars...

Till you remember how lately you were made, and how wonderful it was when you came into it: and more rejoice in the palace of your glory, than if it had been made but today morning.

Thomas Traherne

Do you not know that your body is a temple of the indwelling Holy Spirit?

1 Corinthians 6:19 (REB)

There are no souls without bodies. God alone is wholly without body.

Gottfried Wilhelm Leibniz

36 Gender Wars...

Sexy People?

The psychologist Deborah Tannen has researched one of the major, but usually neglected, differences between men and women: the difference in the way they talk to one another. Her claims ring true...

A couple are driving down a motorway. The woman says: 'Do you want to stop for lunch at the next service station?' The man says, 'No.' Twenty minutes later they are into a well-worn row about nothing in particular. Why?

According to Tannen it is partly because women don't speak, or even ask questions, just to get information, as men tend to do. The question in the car is an 'invitation to intimacy', that is an opening move in what was meant to be a *conversation*, a discussion, a

185

sharing of thoughts and hopes. But the man responded as if he were still at work, and had been asked if he needed a left-hand threaded grunge pin or whether he knew the price of pig-iron in Tokyo.

Women (often) do not just speak to convey neutral facts across intervening spaces; men (often) do. Women speak in order to talk, and talk in order to share a relationship. When they complain that men don't understand them, it is partly because men don't understand *that*. So...

Twenty minutes later: 'What do you mean, I never want to take you out any more? It was only a ruddy service station.'

'It's not the service station. You just don't understand.'

'Understand what...?'

Gender wars

The battle of the sexes started a long time ago and still it rages, from playground name-calling to marital strife, from tabloid stereotypes ('blonde, playful Sharon', 'rugged, one-of-the-lads Darren') to debates over the political correctness of the minutes of university committees. ('Could it be noted that we shall "person" the departmental stall at the postgraduate fair this year, madam chair?').

Battles are the products of deep feelings, and men and women certainly arouse deep feelings in one another: passionate attraction, deep intimate love—*and* sometimes contemptuous hatred. You are more likely to be murdered by the person who has agreed to share your life at its most profound level than by anyone else. Sex—and 'gender'—has an ugly head, always ready to be raised.

But, of course, sex is essential to the continuation of human life. Not even couch potatoes can propagate themselves without a partner on the couch. And sexual love is surely one of the most fulfilling and natural of human experiences. Admittedly some Christians down the centuries have argued for the superiority of

186

a celibate life, and others have conspired with sub-Christian social and political forces to oppress women, particularly married women and mothers. But Christianity at its best recognizes the equality before God of the sexes, and the God-given nature of sex and marriage. As the Anglican wedding service puts it, marriage 'is given, that with delight and tenderness [husband and wife] may know each other in love, and, through the joy of their bodily union, may strengthen the union of their hearts and lives'.

However, being the sort of men and women that we are, we are likely to fall from this high calling from time to time and end up hating whoever we loved the most. Or at least we find that intimacy (which is just a particularly close sort of 'familiarity') can 'breed contempt', along with other offspring. Men and women can certainly be—or at least appear—very contemptuous of one another, not least in conversations between the sexes.

Power and which people?
In recent times some churches have been split over the question of the ordination of women. Pragmatic and theological questions aside, the debates reveal a concern about the location and exercise of *power*. The fundamental question, as so often, is: who runs this show, then? Within Christianity there is a spectrum of answers on offer, from a serious commitment to equality to an insistence on the biblical rule of the subordination of women to men (or at least of married women to their husbands).

Some twenty years ago, as a very junior clergyman, I passed on to my bishop the request from a group of female confirmation candidates in their twenties and thirties. They wanted to be able to kneel before him as the male confirmands did, without being encumbered by the unsightly white headscarf traditionally provided by the diocese just for them. My letter was, I thought, carefully argued: theologically, pastorally, psychologically and politically. In due course I got the reply: 'Tell them that it is done for the sake of seemliness, and I'm sure they will understand.' They didn't and nor did I; but it is interesting that even then there was no attempt to quote Paul's views on women covering their heads in church or even to appeal to church tradition.

(Admittedly, that would have been risky, for the baptism-confirmations of the early church involved *all* the candidates wearing white.) However, the bishop's response used a word that smacked of propriety, good taste, respectability—that is, order. Apparently the women had to be tamed and their hair had to be controlled, lest it and they burst out uncontrollably in front of the altar.

This is all very odd, but it will not seem unfamiliar to many women. Religious men have often acted and spoken as if their piety had to be protected against the temptations of the other sex. Perhaps this is a form of pornography (see Chapter 44): treating women as objects (or subjects?) of sexual temptation, rather than as persons—religious individuals in their own right. It is no wonder that so many feminist theologians have criticized the marginalization of women down the centuries of church history.

Women are not there 'for men', as men are not there 'for women', but to be Christians—and Christian leaders—in their own right.

Which brings us back to power. At least the bishop I wrote to replied. A couple of years before I had written to a magazine in another diocese criticizing an article by an (unmarried) residential canon who argued against the ordination of women on the grounds that a married clergywoman would have to obey her husband's wishes, for example about where they should live, and could not therefore exercise full responsibility in a church. Is that, I asked, what marriage is really supposed to be like?

This time there was no response. The canon's argument was just as bizarre as the bishop's, and in the end suffers from the same myopic perception of the proper relationships between the sexes. If *marriage* is about order through power—line-management—then disaster is around the corner for both men and women. If the *church* is about ordering people about, obeying and being obeyed, then we should certainly try to be clear about who does the obeying and who obeys. But in that case disaster is around the corner for the church also.

Of course women can and do exercise power, and not just in boardrooms and educational institutions. There is no bar to it in families and churches either. But they *shouldn't* operate in that way there, and for the same reason that the men shouldn't: because it is inappropriate, improper and destructive of love. If priesthood is about power, then it is not priesthood. If sexual relationships—relations between the sexes—are about power, then they are not relationships.

The proper exercise of power in churches, as in families, is shown by the power that in the end is found most often in weakness (see Chapter 19), and revealed best in a tormented figure pinned to a cross. After all crucified power, for men as well as women, is the only power that is permitted in the Kingdom of God.

37 Humour...

Serious People?

Funny thing—humour. Animals don't seem to go in for it much. You don't see cats slapping their thighs and roaring with mirth. Dogs don't tell many jokes, or laugh when their owners step in the whoopsie in their bare feet.

Humour is not the same thing as play, of course. Animals certainly play. Two lion cubs roll around mock-scrapping with biting, gouging, ear-pulling and no holds barred. But despite the fur flying and claws scratching neither seems to get hurt. We recognize it as playfulness, though even here there's just the suspicion that they are really training for the time when they will kill in earnest.

But humour? Animals seem not to understand jokes, puns or limericks. Even the laughing hyena doesn't really see the funny side of life. And as for fish... well!

Banana-skins

Human beings are radically different. We seem to have invented humour. And this fact in itself is worth brooding over. What is it about us that makes us capable of spotting the odd, quirky, incongruous aspects of our existence and then finding them amusing?

Kierkegaard said that 'humour is always a concealed pair'. I suppose he meant that humour trades on the unexpected collision of two different worlds. It works like this: here are two independent events or two independent ideas. They have two different meanings—there is nothing funny about that—but they have these meanings *at the same time*. The point at which these two worlds touch is the flash-point for laughter. We can see this at work even in the most hackneyed jokes. For example:

> 'Waiter, waiter, what's this soup?'
> 'It's bean soup, sir.'
> 'I don't care what it's been. What is it now?'

> 'I bought this dog going cheap.'
> 'That's funny. They usually go woof.'

> 'Doctor, my son doesn't want to go to school.'
> 'He may have school phobia. When did it first begin?'
> 'About the time when he was made deputy head.'

The hearer is making smooth progress along a particular track when—whoosh—the ground opens and he or she is unceremoniously dumped onto a lower level. Humour is dislocation of the safe, taken-for-granted world. Confronted with a universe which won't quite stay still while we organize it, we have no recourse but to laugh. We are let down, but quite enjoy the experience.

All of which may be something of a parable. Human beings are aware even in their jokes that life has a way of upsetting their best-laid schemes.

> *Keep Britain tidy.*
> *Kill a tourist.*

Earn cash in your spare time.
Blackmail your friends.

Preserve wildlife.
Pickle a squirrel today.

Adventures in two worlds

The idea of two parallel worlds is illustrated by the way the ancient world viewed puns. We find puns corny, fit for a groan. The ancients were fascinated by the fact that the same word could live in two worlds at the same time. In a mysterious way the word was a doorway from either world into the other. Out there is another world, walking along step by step, never touching this world, except now and again, at the point of collision. The cat, locked into the world of the mundane, has no sense of humour because it is never aware of encountering any world other than the mundane. The human being is always a creature of this world *and* the other. Humour is an odd way of pointing towards this fact.

> *A quirky, facetious old colonel*
> *Whose humour was frankly infernal*
>   *said, 'My jokes may be sad*
>   *and incredibly bad*
> *but suggest that my nature's eternal.'*

Serious laughter

The jump from limericks to God may seem a preposterous one. But the way in which humour points beyond the here and now can be seen most clearly when humour mocks what is apparently deadly serious. According to those who survived the Nazi death camps, it was laughter which kept the spirit alive. To make a joke when you are confronted with an evil presence which holds the power of life and death over you is to make a statement about where true power lies. In the light of the joke the relative nature of what might seem like absolute tyranny is shown up. St Laurence met his death as a martyr by being roasted on a grid iron. He said, 'Turn me over. I'm done on this side.'

This is a clear assertion that ultimate power does not rest with the torturer. Citizens of that other world can afford to laugh at the posturings of those who live only in this world and thus delude themselves. Humour is a declaration of *hope*. Humour performs a similar role for ourselves. We are also capable of supposing ourselves to be rather bigger than our boots. To be able to laugh at yourself is to allow yourself to be put in your place. Exactly in your place. Self-rejection is neither funny nor constructive. But self-mockery is affectionate, objective and a great help towards humility.

Francis of Assisi and his companion Masseo arrived at a crossroads when on a journey. Having no idea which way to go they turned round and round like tops until they were dizzy. Then they staggered off down the road which faced them. The moral seems to be: God holds the whole world in his hand; it doesn't do to be over-serious when you are out on God's business.

Humour can deflate our pride (do you have to be so pompous? Remember you are a human being under God). Humour can dispel our self-humiliation (do you have to grovel quite so much? You are not a worm; you are a human being under God). Karl Barth, the great theologian, observed that the contrast between humans and the honour done to them by God is too great for us to take ourselves 'ceremoniously'.

This is not so different from the advice given to an eighteen-year-old university entrant facing her college interviewers and anticipating the ordeal with some apprehension. 'Just think of them in their underpants.'

Humour is what saves us all.

Caricaturist Ralph Sallon

38 Raiders of the Lost Ark Again...

Complicated People?

It's not too easy to escape Christmas. Even the *Sunday Times* Nervous Breakdown Chart gives it twenty points. Just experiencing Christmas, you note, not a bad Christmas or that utterly horrendous Christmas when you threw the Christmas tree across the room and dumped all their presents on the pavement—just a straightforward, holly and mistletoe, chestnut stuffing and *Guns of Navarone* Christmas takes you twenty points nearer having to have a quiet lie-down for three months.

Christmas has still got something to do with religion—just. Not just *Raiders of the Lost Ark* but school nativity plays, not just Rudolph the red-nosed reindeer but carols by candlelight. It *is* a festival of the winter solstice, the Roman Saturnalia and the office party; it is also a celebration of the incarnation of God.

To put it that way, 'incarnation of God', is to raise the stakes somewhat. The language of serious theology is a little out of fashion. Some modern carols prefer to talk of 'Mary's boy-child', or even 'little donkey on a dusty road'. The older carols, rather more heavyweight, pulled no punches.

> *Veiled in flesh the Godhead see,*
> *Hail the incarnate Deity,*
> *Pleased as man with man to dwell,*
> *Jesus our Emmanuel.*

God and human—does this language make sense? And, even if it does, what does it matter? There is a natural impatience with making things unnecessarily complicated. The Christmas story is a good tale with a strong storyline—why drag in gobbledygook about incarnation?

Old square circles

No one is pretending that the language is easy. But it's important to appreciate that the first Christians were not being perverse spoilsports. They were sure that Jesus was a real man; they were equally positive that they had encountered the Divine in him. In a rather impressive way they were determined to try to make sense of these two conflicting facts rather than take the easy way out and collapse one or the other. It's a bit like trying to square the circle.

But can you in fact square the circle? In one way combining different natures in one reality is not difficult. A dress can be short, red *and* expensive. A book can be leather-bound, boring and long. But can you combine such different natures as divinity (infinite, uncreated, everlasting, pure spirit) and humanity (limited, created, mortal, flesh and blood)? Can God have a birthday? Human beings can. And where do you start? From the God end? But never quite able to accept that he was completely human? Or from the human end? And never really believing that he was God? God and human: well, which is he? A bit of both? All one and none of the other? Seeming to be one but really being the other—like the nineteenth Earl of Loamshire dressed up as a tramp?

Now with ancient theologies of Christ the early Christians tried, essentially, to think of some way of putting two billiard balls on the same spot at the same time! They were never able to leave the question alone, and each theory had its own jargon:

❏ Adoptionism saw Jesus as an ordinary person who was adopted later by God (at his baptism or resurrection) and made Lord and Christ.

❏ Docetism is the reverse: Jesus only 'appeared' to be human and 'seemed' to suffer and die. He was *really* God wearing

195

humanity like a guest at a fancy dress party. (Valentinus boldly declared: 'Thus Jesus exercised his divinity: he ate and drank in a peculiar manner, not evacuating his food.')

❏ Kenoticism presented a middle way: seeing Christ as pre-existent in heaven but 'emptying himself of all but love' during his earthly life, only to be exalted again to his previous power, knowledge and so on at the end.

❏ Nestorianism viewed Christ as an aggregate of component parts, the human bit and the God bit existing side by side like a bundle of sticks glued together or grains of barley and wheat mixed in a sack but not actually running into one another.

All were honest attempts to describe a mystery.

❏ Incarnation became the 'agreed version'. The son of God brought all his divine nature into the world and took his human nature back into heaven. The Council of Chalcedon (AD 451) affirmed that Jesus was both 'truly God' and 'truly human' and that these two natures were perfectly combined in 'one person'. They existed 'without confusion', 'without change', 'without division' and 'without separation', as wine once added to water can be detected in every drop. Part of this theological dispute has been called 'the argument about an iota', because the phrase 'of one substance with God' (homoousios) is only one letter (in Greek the letter iota) different from 'of similar substance' (homoiousios—or a bit like God).

Of course, it does not take long to see that the official line isn't an *explanation*—it's more a way of safeguarding all the elements so as to make sure that none gets lost. It's an agreement that this is the way that we need to go on talking about Jesus, even if it gives us a headache.

New square circles

Modern attempts at a satisfactory 'Christology' have tended to split between the functional and the ontological—between what Jesus does and who he is. In the former Christ is God because he *functions* like, or does the work of, God. He is the medium through which God expresses himself. He is like a magnifying glass focusing the rays of the sun. In the latter, Jesus is 'divine stuff'. It is not just that he does the work of God; he has God's nature (or essence) in him. He *is* what he does and *does* what he is.

Does it matter which line you take? Those who hold to the ontological view—which is the traditional and orthodox one—say it does. For it makes Christ unique. He is not to be reduced to a prophet, saint, 'good man' or great teacher. It is proper to worship him. Since he is God, his forgiveness is truly God's work. Since he really is human he knows from the inside what it is to be human. A God who will voluntarily live a human life (like a human being opting to become an ant) tells us something important, distinctive and profoundly reassuring about what God is like.

The matter has been put rather neatly in these words: 'In order to *save* us, he has to be God. In order to save *us*, he has to be one of us'—genuinely human. 'He became as we are in order that we might become like him,' as Paul put it.

At Christmas time it is, of course, easier to stick with 'little donkey'; but, in the end, it's much less of a pick-me-up.

39 Still Breathing After All These Years...

Hopeful People?

Easter has never caught on as Christmas has. The shops do their best, with the promise of the Easter Bunny bringing enough eggs to satisfy even those in the advanced stages of the give-me-chocolate-or-I-die disease. We have a new game show on TV and a lot of old films. In Britain summer fashions fill the shops, the sound of the lawnmower is heard in the land, and people complain once again that the church won't agree to a fixed date for Easter so that we go on freezing one year and roasting the next. But it's never, as you might say, 'caught on'. A holiday weekend and that's it.

Which is a little strange. Because if there's a message that our world might want, or need to hear, it ought to be the Easter one. 'Love is come again like wheat that springeth green.' But maybe that kind of language only touches the heart when you sit by a hospital bed or stand by an open grave, feeling that terrible mixture of grief, loss, anger, fear and possibly guilt, knowing that someone you love has gone for good and will 'come no more—no, never, never, never...'

Certainly, Christianity is about Jesus' resurrection almost to the point of excess. Everything in it points towards this truth and flows from it. As the Pope has said, 'We are an Easter people and hallelujah is our song.' Without the hope which issues from the resurrection Christianity ends in disaster and Christians are 'of all people the most miserable'.

The gate of life eternal?

But is it possible to take the idea seriously? People die so finally. You can see the life go out of them. Just the husk is left. Is there any reason to suppose that it was different with Jesus? Or that in any sensible way, we can look for life outside the wooden box in the hole in the ground?

It is, of course, important to recognize what resurrection is not. No one is arguing for the recovery of consciousness, as if Jesus had revived having been in a coma. Nor are they describing the resuscitation of a corpse—a kind of second Lazarus who came back to life after some unusual out-of-the-body experience—the sort of story *Reader's Digest* runs under the heading, 'Fresh Evidence about the Other Side.' What is at stake is resurrection—the transmutation of the body into the spiritual realm, an altogether different and totally unimaginable mode of existence.

In the Gospels we can see the disciples wrestling with this mind-blowing concept. They are sure that the risen Jesus is not a ghost. He eats before their gaze. Yet he is not subject to the restrictions of time and space, for locked doors cannot keep him out. He is clearly the same Jesus, known to all, bearing the marks of the crucifixion. Yet he is strangely unrecognizable to Mary mourning by his tomb and the two disciples who walk with him on the way to Emmaus. It is the same Jesus whom they have followed for three years and yet not exactly the same—something momentous has happened to him.

For most Christians this miracle involves an empty tomb. Indeed many books about the resurrection never get far beyond the Whodunnit? point. 'Who moved the stone?' is the key question and the reader is taken through a list of possible explanations—the disciples or tomb robbers stole the body; the authorities removed it for safe-keeping; Jesus was in a coma and never really died; the women disciples went to the wrong tomb; everybody was suffering from hallucinations. Each theory is shown in turn to be unlikely or impossible so that the resurrection of Jesus remains as the only convincing explanation.

A conjuring trick with bones?

Some Christians have resisted this route. In the 1980s David Jenkins, Bishop of Durham, in what became known as 'The Durham Affair' roundly declared that the resurrection was 'more than a conjuring trick with bones'. For him as for other Christians, 'Christ is risen', but Jenkins holds that it was Jesus' resurrected or immortal spirit which appeared to the disciples, his body not being raised to life at all.

Now of course an empty grave does not constitute a resurrection. But it is still worth asking whether 'matter matters' (see also Chapter 35). Certainly Christian documents assert that the tomb was empty and the attack on Christianity assumed it. Perhaps also plausibility requires it, since the Easter faith would have had difficulty in gaining purchase in a city where there was an identifiable grave containing the bones of Jesus.

But does matter matter that much? Those who think it does will argue that for the resurrection to be the sign of the New Age, God must do something about the flesh of Jesus. Given that death is so obviously about bodies, how can *the* sign that death is defeated ignore bodies? How can it take place independently of the dead body, as if it were somehow irrelevant? After all, the corpse is the primary evidence that something has gone seriously wrong. They will argue that it is exactly God's style to come into the situation, work within it and transform it. It is not his way to ignore the problem and set up shop somewhere else.

So what?

All this raises the question of the meaning of the resurrection. It may well be an act of God but what is its point? There are a number of answers. First, since for the Jews resurrection was what would happen at the end of time, it marked the beginning of the New Age, the end-time, the turning point of the worlds. But it was also seen as the guarantee in advance of what God would do at the end of history. Moreover, it vindicated the life of Jesus: the apparent failure, the convicted blasphemer was now established as Lord and Messiah. The incentive for reinterpreting his crucifixion came from this. Good Friday could not now be a disaster.

These implications are equally true for contemporary Christians. They too declare that Christ is risen and that he is alive in them and in the world. They too look forward to their own resurrection since Jesus is the first sheaf of a harvest to come. They too rejoice in the prospect of a redeemed creation and the defeat of death.

Belonging

'Community' is a modern buzz-word,
but communities are made up of
individuals relating to one another—
or pointedly ignoring each other if
communications have broken down.
How *do* we deal with others, and does
that say anything about how we might
deal with God?

40 Let's Play Out...

The Friend?

Dear ~~Dairy~~ Diary

Got up. Had breakfast. Muesli-puke again, yuk! Nearly late for school bus again. Mum mad again.

Forgot homework. Old Rogers mad again.

<u>Horrible</u> Maths. 3 out of 20 for test. Rained for games. Mr Smith seemed to enjoy it! Got wet through. Pete and Jake and me played this great game after school in the park. I got caught most, but still great. Jake did this magic impression of Miss Sherman with a football up his jersey! Decided to go a bike ride together on Sat on the railway line.

NEED: sandwiches (peanut butter and Marmite)
            Cokes
            Dad's map (nick from his desk Friday)
            Simon's bike (blackmail him into letting me Thursday)

Home late. Mum mad again. Tuna salad for tea <u>again</u>. Said it tasted like ***! Mum mad again! Mum mad with Dad for laughing. Dad mad again! No TV! Fascists!!

Homework—crummy maths, boring history. Sewed up hole in trousers so Mum wouldn't notice. She did! Mad again!!! Had to go to bed early. This house is a police state.

Good day though. Can't stop laughing at Jake's impressions. Pete had a great joke about Mr Wilson. He said...

Mum just been in to see why I was laughing. Mad again!! Don't adults enjoy anything?

Befriending

Friends make all the difference.

When I was ten I was approached by a new boy at school with a very direct, very un-British question, 'Will you be my friend?' Being only ten, and only British (and only male), the only response was a sort of very embarrassed, almost non-committal agreement, delivered in a voice that probably expressed quite the opposite.

In fact over the next eight years we did become good friends. But that was nothing to do with the original encounter, couched in the ritual language almost of a proposal. It just happened that we developed common concerns, and walked a common road—and caught the same bus. As C.S. Lewis writes, 'those who are going nowhere can have no fellow-travellers'. We went to the same schools, and studied in the end almost the same subjects. But we were very unlike each other.

Friends are often very different. The common element between them is somehow not in them, but beyond them. The real question in friendship, according to Lewis, is 'Do you see the same truth?'

Being a friend

Friendship is often underrated, partly because being 'just good friends' is seen as an alternative to more intimate relationships between the sexes. But friendship, even in marriage, can be the most relational of relationships, with a closeness that allows the other the freedom to be her- or himself.

According to the philosopher Donald Evans *friendliness* is 'a readiness and willingness to risk the self by... giving and receiving at a very deep personal level'. He writes that a friend is someone who confirms me: 'I feel that he is *with* me, *for* me.' But a friend may also confront me, challenging me to be the best that I can be—without condemning my vices or inadequacies. Above all friendliness *celebrates* the strengths of another person for their own sake: 'If I look on someone as a close friend, I celebrate his very existence.' This leads to a commitment to one's friends, a respect for their privacy and freedom, and a real affection for them.

Friends are great for borrowing from: coffee, books, ideas, a car ride or a fiver. The true friend is generous, and expects no tally of debts to be kept. But in true friendship the books eventually do balance, at least if the auditors are the friends themselves. It is not a matter of a lunch for a lunch, but of 'to each according to their need; from each according to their strengths'.

Is this, then, a sort of communism? If so, it is one like that of the early church, when in the first flush of what they called 'fellowship' they created a community in which, according to the Book of Acts, 'all things were held in common'. Friends share; their unity is a common unity.

Obviously we are friends with a person because we get something out of the relationship. At the very least, we enjoy their company. But this interested affection, in which we have and find an 'interest' (something for us) is heavily qualified in true friendship. True friendship has a disinterested element too. This is not a matter of being '*uninterested*', but—as the dictionary puts it—of being 'not influenced by one's own advantage'. We celebrate the very existence of our friends, for *their* sake, not ours.

Friend of friends

The philosopher H. H. Price argued that the way in which we 'believe in' our friends—that is are in favour of them, 'for' them, trust them—is our best analogy for believing in God. As soon as we start thanking God for his gifts, 'being grateful for them with a gratitude which is not just a lively sense of favours to come', Price writes, our belief in God ceases to be wholly interested. We are beginning now to value God for his own sake, and to believe that it is a good thing—good in itself—that God exists and is what he is.

The nearest analogy to this is our belief in a friend, 'where there is a similar combination of interested and disinterested believing-in'. It is perhaps significant, Price adds, that some mystics have referred to God as 'The Friend'.

It is a high calling to be a friend. The highest calling, Christians would claim, is to be called to be a friend of God. Of course being friends with God cannot be the same as being friends with a human being. But there is an analogy. Donald Evans again:

> *I trust that God confronts, and celebrates his human friends, treating each with devotion, respect and affection... The relation is not like that between an infant and his mother. It is more like that between two adult friends.*
>
> *In so far as I am friendly towards God I confirm his existence, acknowledging that he is distinct from me— indeed he is the very 'ground' on which I stand. I confront God, calling him to task for many of the injustices and tragedies of human life... I celebrate God's existence in worship, devote myself to him in loyalty and attention, respectfully refrain from trying to manipulate his power, and affectionately seek closeness with him by being close to his creatures.*

Thank God for friends: intimates that give us insight into the Intimate, companions who remind us of a greater.

41 Partly Political...

The Neighbour?

Moving house, they say, is nearly as traumatic a
psychological experience as divorce, and not far behind
bereavement.

Remember the last time? And meeting the neighbour
who is going to be very hard to love?

*Hello, my name is Mrs Wallace. I'm your neighbour on the
other side: the detached house, with the separate garage.
I just wondered if you would like some tea. I know what it
can be like moving in. Doing it on your own, I see. No
husband, perhaps? Yes there are a lot like that nowadays,
though mainly at the cheaper end of the estate. Was that
your little boy? Well, perhaps he will be less rude when he
has settled down. I'll just put the tray on the stairs. It
won't matter if it spills there, you'll be getting new carpets
soon, no doubt.*

*Now we're very friendly around here, apart from the young
couple opposite—but they are slighly common, from the
North probably, and he put up a poster once: Save the
Whale or Stop the Poll Tax. Something rather vulgar. But
Mrs Burton is very nice. Her son is a doctor and her
husband was in the army. An officer, of course, one of the
better regiments. And Mr Ayleshire is Neighbourhood
Watch. Sort of runs it. Very keen. Does a lot for charity:
committee work, of course, not door to door. Dogs mainly,
and Distressed Gentlefolk. Not those foreign ones. (Of
course, those black babies are very sad, but it's the parents
I blame, don't you?)*

*I hope I'm not in the way here, I see the men have nearly
finished. Perhaps your husband has the better furniture? I
can recommend a good window-cleaner. Your predecessor*

never used one, I'm afraid. Rather a slovenly Madam, I thought. Some of the washing! And the children weren't checked at all. The things they said to me.

There are some nice schools nearby: fee-paying, but you get what you pay for in education. These comprehensive teachers just don't make enough to be really devoted. Don't you agree?

Well if you think you really can manage, I will be off. Take care of the tea-set, won't you? One can't get the pieces now, but it's so much nicer than beakers. I do hope you settle in quickly. Oh, and did I say, you do know that you can't keep hens here?

Beggar the neighbours

All made up, of course, apart from the reference to comprehensive teachers (from a conversation with the daughter of an independent school head) and the advice about hens (shouted across the gardens from a next-door-neighbour-but-one to my surprised parents when they last moved house).

Most neighbours are good neighbours. Some are saints. But a few seem to delight in destroying any possibility of a friendly, give-and-take relationship.

It matters what neighbours are like. In the Old Testament a fair bit of fuss is made about the neighbour who shifts the boundary stones, or casts a covetous eye on your cattle—or your spouse. In the New Testament Jesus himself is asked to answer the question, 'Who is my neighbour?' In the towns and cities in which most of us live, getting on with neighbours can mean the difference between contentment and misery, for here the neighbour is just across the fence or just on the other side of a thin, sound-transmitting, party wall.

'Living in community' lies at the heart of social and political life. We *have* to live together. To do this we very often have to give up our individual rights and wants for the sake of others. It's bad enough when you are related to these others. You can choose your friends, they say, but you can't choose your family. And unfortunately only the very, very rich can *really* pick and choose their neighbours.

So here we are: cheek by jowl, in the big city or the small village, often not feeling very neighbourly. But we are stuck with them, usually one on each side, a few across the road peering through the curtains, and the couple over the back hedge with a greenhouse cunningly placed so as to attract the kids' footballs.

It is tempting to begin in a new house by building up the boundary walls, sound-proofing the place and electrifying the fences. 'I keep myself to myself' can then be our proud boast. 'Neither a borrower nor a lender (at least of lawn-mowers) shall I be.' Our home can be our castle, and so can our city, or our nation. We can forget the neighbours. Can't we?

Belonging

Fat chance. Only the mentally ill and the millionaire can get away with such isolation. The Neighbourhood Watch comes in many shapes and forms. If my neighbours *don't* ring the police when they see my house broken into, or offer advice or help when they see me struggling with the car or the drains, then my property will suffer, and I shall suffer with it. I *need* such neighbourliness, and not just because I need practical help. I need someone to show that they care. It doesn't have to be a lot; often we are happier if it is not too much. A little neighbouring goes a long way.

There is no more dreadful obituary than 'no one cared'. 'He died, and no one cared.' 'Not even the neighbours noticed.' What really converted Scrooge was seeing how the neighbours would react to his death.

We need to belong somewhere enough to be noticed; to be that much a part of a community, a street, a world; to belong to one another at least that much.

In Lennon and McCartney's 'Eleanor Rigby', one of their most poignant ballads, Eleanor ('lives in a dream... waits by the window') and Father McKenzie ('darning his socks in the night when there's nobody there') represent 'all the lonely people'. The song asks *the* significant question about their position in our great scheme of things: 'Where do they all belong?'

It is a rhetorical question. Patently they belong nowhere. But their isolation is our loss. 'We must love one another or die,' wrote W. H. Auden. At the very least we must love one another enough so that our neighbours do not die, literally or psychologically. For in their deaths we shall lose something of ourselves.

Politics and salvation
Hence Christianity is about politics too. For politics is about people: communities, neighbours, living together. In the great parable of the Last Judgment in Matthew's Gospel 'all the nations' are judged not by their beliefs or their churchgoing, but by their neighbourliness.

The righteous are righteous because they fed, visited, clothed and gave a home to Christ. They are very surprised: 'Lord, when was it that we saw you hungry and fed you, or thirsty and gave you drink, a stranger and took you home, or naked and clothed you? When did we see you ill or in prison, and come to see you?'

The answer we know well, but we don't really believe it. 'Truly, I tell you: anything you did for one of these, however insignificant, you did for me.'

The story of the Bible, it is often said, begins with two people in a garden (the Eden of Genesis), but ends with a city (the New Jerusalem of Revelation) and a crowd 'greater than any can number'. It looks as though we might have to get used to living together.

(Oh, and she was right: you *couldn't* keep hens there.)

> No man is an island, entire of itself; every man is a piece of the continent, a part of the main... Any man's death diminishes me, because I am involved in Mankind...
>
> John Donne

> Those who say we should keep the Bible out of politics worry me. Which Bible are they reading? The Bible I know speaks of a God involved in this world.
>
> Archbishop Desmond Tutu

42 The Other Cheek...

The Peacemaker?

The roots of aggression and violence lie within all of us. You don't have to be in a war to retaliate. Any two-year-old will demonstrate how to pinch and bite when thwarted. And all over the country on Saturday nights the young braves of the tribe lash themselves into a lather of macho violence. In 1992 Vinny Jones the footballer was fined heavily by the Football Association for bringing the game into disrepute. He had produced a video which brought to light the hundreds of dirty tricks employed by professional footballers when the referee isn't looking. There was something profoundly shocking about cataloguing behaviour that everyone saw Saturday by Saturday. Perhaps it was the degree of cynicism that appalled the authorities. Everyone knows footballers aren't angels, but lessons in how to rake your studs down your opponent's calf seemed altogether too calculating.

The highway code?

But it takes cars to bring out the worst in people. Once in a car some people are transformed into Mad Max or Boadicea with scythes on the wheels of the chariot. Can you imagine eight Beatitudes for the victims of bad drivers?

Blessed are you when they practically drive up your exhaust.

Blessed are you when they drive towards you with their lights on full beam.

Blessed are you when they park on double yellow lines and completely block the road for ten minutes while they post their letters and chat to passers-by.

Blessed are you when they go up on the outside lane on the approach to roadworks and cut in just before the first cone, waving cheerily at you as if you had let them in, while you have apoplexy.

Blessed are you when they drive behind you on motorways flashing their lights because you are taking a microsecond too long to overtake the lorry.

Blessed are you when they put nodding dogs, woollen dice and rude and abusive stickers in the rear window.

Blessed are you when they join motorways regardless of other traffic and expect you to pull over into the outside lane despite the juggernaut which is overtaking you at 98 mph.

Blessed are you when they cut you up and then have the cheek to put two fingers up as they scream off into the distance.

Losing face

Of course aggression can show itself in subtler ways. Arm wrestling does not always require physical contact. You've only got to listen to some committees to see that two of the members are scoring points regardless of the agenda. The third is locked into a brooding silence that chills the atmosphere. Here at the end of the table a wet blanket raises points of principle without end, effectively blocking any useful work, while the chairman is bulldozing, steamrollering, railroading his points through the opposition as ruthlessly as a linebacker for the Chicago Bears. Verbal aggression—active or passive—can be more difficult to handle than a slap in the face.

It's as if there is some in-built calculator that tells you whether you are down or up on the 'honour' scale. If my honour is impugned (what a splendidly pompous word), I am bound to redress the balance—that is, get my own back—as if you'd stolen something from me and I had to send out a posse to reclaim it. I can 'lose face', but if I do I need to get it back—that is, recover the mask of dignity which has been temporarily knocked askew. In fact the very phrase 'lose face' comes from a Chinese custom of covering your face with a fan when you were embarrassed or humiliated.

All this makes the teaching of Jesus seem positively unnatural. 'Turning the other cheek' is 'losing face' in a big way and deliberately. 'Loving your enemies' keeps them at the top of the see-saw and if they're up, then you must be down. What's so special about the meek and mild? It is just possible that you will inherit the earth but only if the rest of us decide to let you. As a model for living, the peacemaker and non-retaliator doesn't get off the ground. Where else would you expect to find a doormat?

Turning the other cheek

Jesus himself doesn't fit this picture. Most of the time he is the opposite of a doormat: assertive, direct, challenging. He protests rather than stays silent; a controversialist in dispute, rather than a yes-man.

This kind of aggression—if that is the right word for it—can be enormously valuable. Contending for the faith has taken Christians into the most hostile situations and led them to speak the truth even at risk to their lives. Those standing up for the weak and powerless may well need to be fired by anger. Abraham Lincoln is supposed to have seen an example of slavery and declared, 'I'll hit that and I'll hit it hard.' The military hymns, 'Onward Christian Soldiers' and all that, are not just the product of British imperialism. Contempt for the old and frail, the torture and maiming of those who cannot defend themselves, sexual abuse of children, wanton cruelty towards dumb animals, corruption of the innocent, all spark off a savage indignation. The image of Christ with the whip of cords touches the imagination because in some circumstances anything less than anger would constitute a failure in being human.

But where then do we get the contrary image of 'Gentle Jesus, meek and mild', and what are we to make of it? If it doesn't come from mawkish Victorian piety, then perhaps it owes its existence to the Jesus of the trial which condemned him to death. Here is a suffering servant, the archetypical victim, mocked, ridiculed, humiliated and apparently too cowed to fight back. No protest comes from his lips. He fails to swear at his persecutors. The thief on the cross seems to have taken a nobler line. They might crucify him but at least they couldn't break his spirit.

This is a monumentally wrong reading of what is going on. And it takes us into the heart of the 'turn the other cheek' saying. For it is only the person who is utterly secure and in charge who can endure ill-treatment and absorb it. To return the blow ensures that evil continues, cannoning off one object on to another like a snooker ball. As Tevye in the musical *Fiddler on the Roof* says, 'an eye for an eye and a tooth for a tooth. And so the whole world ends up toothless and blind.' But to absorb the hurt deliberately and as the result of a decision of the will is to draw its sting. The mother who gathers up into her arms the screaming and kicking two-year-old shows maturity, dignity, control and love, even while she is being struck and shouted at. The adult who strikes back in uncontrollable rage descends to the level of the child.

43 Rules, Rules, Rules...

The Lawmaker?

Most people think of religion as a set of rules. The Ten Commandments encourage this with their repeated 'Thou shalt not...' As one child said, 'They don't help you to be good and they just put ideas into your head.' St Paul made a similar point when he complained, 'I really wasn't that interested in coveting, until I read that I shouldn't be doing it.'

The Christian dynamic is the reverse of what is usually accepted. You don't set out by trying to be good, even the words 'righteous', 'law-abiding', 'rectitude', sound like a strait-jacket. Virtue, if we must use the word, is a *response* to the way God has treated us. Paul's letters often spend three or four chapters telling his readers about the amazing way

God loves us before he gets to the 'therefore... this is the way you should be behaving.'

The feel-good factor

Here Christianity seems to have hit on a universal experience. We *are* good when we *feel* good. When we are happy with ourselves. When I feel valued, affirmed, cherished, when my self-esteem and self-image are so high they're nearly off the scale, then I am capable of astounding acts of generosity, altruism and care. Conversely, when someone puts me down with an acid criticism of my appearance, intelligence, and general standing as a human being, then I go home and kick the cat.

Christian Ethics does have rules, of course. But they should be seen more as a framework and a guide, examples of the freaky things love might get up to at any moment rather than a list of regulations to be followed to the letter.

In fact the life that is rule-governed can often feel restricted. C.S. Lewis wrote of 'the woman who lives for others' and added, 'You can tell the others by their hunted look.'

Sometimes the pursuit of virtue leads to a sense of strain. 'Have I done enough?' or 'What will they think of me?' Goodness becomes a matter of achievement, with a series of attainment targets to be met. Sometimes it can lead to an elaborate calculation of profit and loss. 'Do we owe them a meal?' and 'I don't want to be beholden to them.' Often the focus is on *myself* rather than on *the other*. If you're not sure about this, consider the following dialogue, repeated in a thousand households round about the beginning of December:

A. What about the Richardsons?

B. Did they send to us?

A. Last year, no. The year before, yes. Twice actually.

B. How come twice?

A. Well, I think he sent one before Christmas. Then they got ours, forgot they'd sent one and she sent one to stave off guilt. Arrived just before New Year's Eve.

B. Shall we knock them off the list then?

A. Well, I'd say yes but this will be just the year for them to send one because we sent one last year. Don't want to get caught out.

> *B. Be embarrassing... especially since you're likely to see him at the Centre.*

A. Well, quite.

> *B. What about a present for Nigel?*

A. Well, we've had some really tawdry stuff from him in the past. Isn't there something in the Gift Catalogue–around a tenner?

> *B. Don't you think £10 looks a bit mean?*

A. No, I don't. I only ever get socks or handkerchiefs—or that ghastly calendar thing from some Third World shop. Over the years we must be £30 down. Time to even things up a bit.

> *B. Some kind of gift token then?*

A. Exactly. Or maybe it's worth seeing if he would be happy with 'We won't give to you if you won't give to us.'

Contrast with this the preposterous behaviour of the woman in the Gospel story who poured a box of expensive perfume over Jesus' feet. The gesture is extravagant, spontaneous, unpremeditated and financially ruinous. 'Who cares? It's only money!' seems to be her attitude. Simon, the host, has done the bare minimum to welcome Jesus—perhaps even rather less. Jesus points out the implication. You can tell that she has been forgiven a lot because everything she does shouts out the response of unaffected love and gratitude.

Doing good ought to be natural, an overflowing of the heart, the product of a right relationship. Doing good in this style leads to human flourishing. We grow when we do good in this mode. We all know people who seem incapable of not being generous. They seem to be operating at a more human level as they give us presents, lend books, and invite us to meals.

Christian Ethics is about being touched by God's love and, out of that experience of acceptance, responding with love, warmth and generosity.

Virtue is praised but hated. People run away from it for it is ice-cold and in the world you must keep your feet warm.

Denis Diderot

Love God and do what you like.

Augustine of Hippo

44 It Depends Who's Looking...

The Stranger?

We tend to see sex in everything. A thousand *double-entendres*, and a dozen *Carry On* films prove that. In the old joke, the patient says that every picture the psychiatrist shows him—even those of trees and hens—makes him think of sex. The doctor makes some comments about this. 'Come on,' the client responds, 'you're the one showing the dirty pictures.'

The church sometimes reveals similar hang-ups: fastening only on sexual immorality, and passing over the greater personal and social sins of humankind. You would think sometimes that pornography was more seriously sinful than genocide.

Peeping Tom, Dick... and Harriet?

Pornography, however, is a form of voyeurism; and there is more to that than meets the eye...

Get away from the window, Tom. You know what his lordship said. He'll have your eyes out, if that broken shutter doesn't do it first.

Leave me alone, woman. I've never seen nothing like this, not for middle ages. Not in Coventry anyway.

Disgusting I call it. And insulting to me. You never look at me like that any more. What's she got that I haven't, apart from teeth?

Shut your noise, wench and don't be so medieval-minded. Pure beauty, this is. Never seen nothing like this. Gorgeous blond hair right down to the ground, long shapely legs right up to those round, plump haunches...

Tom! Stop it. Come away at once. It's disgusting. And in a few more centuries I shouldn't be surprised if it won't be recognized as degrading to women as well.

Women, what's this with women? I'm looking at the horse.

Porn and power

It all depends not only on what you're looking at, but on how you are looking. 'Pornography' has been defined as the public exposure of a part of a human being at the expense of the whole. The English word has come down originally from a Greek word referring to a prostitute, someone who sells part of herself (or himself), offering what is only a partial relationship rather than a full relationship with the whole person.

In discussions about pornography, prostitution, obscenity— and even nudity—the conversation usually gets round to treating people as objects (bodies). From a lofty moral height the critic can condemn these activities as 'using people'. This brings us nearer to the heart of the matter, and to a more significant sin.

But you don't have to visit strip clubs or red-light districts to experience that. The philosopher Immanuel Kant put his great principle of practical morality like this:

> *Act in such a way that you always treat every human being, never simply as a means to an end, but always at the same time as an end in himself or herself.*

It is frighteningly easy to use people: to treat them as means to further our own pleasure, success, comfort or plans. Politicians and soldiers find the temptation hard to resist. But so do employers, managers, salespeople, parents and spouses. We all do it. And it denigrates other people, and ourselves with them. To treat people *just* as voters or consumers, or even just as

What do I think about nudity in the cinema? I think you have to be very careful with your ice-cream.

Anon

221

friends-to-me, is to deny that they are people-in-their-own-right, an end in themselves. It is to recognize only a partial person at the expense of the whole.

Value-added

Christian ethics, Christians often need to remind themselves, is largely about valuing people as ends in themselves: individuals of infinite value, 'immortal diamonds'. Jesus overturned conventional values: 'Blessed are the poor'—not the rich; 'Blessed are the meek'—not the proud; the 'first [of this world] shall be last', and so on. The rich, healthy, religious and successful have their rewards already. (What rewards? Why, riches, health and worldly—or churchy—success, of course.) Jesus is physician to the sick. 'The poor' in the psalms and 'the humble' of Mary's song, the Magnificat, are those of low status, those who are 'no people'. They must be *given* the good news that God accepts them; their poverty starkly symbolizes the fact that they could neither afford it nor demand it.

Jesus points to the widow donating two tiny copper coins and tells the disciples that she has given more than any rich donor to the temple treasury. He puts a child in the midst of his followers to present them with a model for being his disciple: someone who is without status. In his words and life Jesus welcomes all who are without social or religious status.

Jesus tries to change the way we value people, especially those whom the world does not value. He would have us see them through his eyes. Or, to shift the metaphor, we must place Jesus between us and them, so that we see them *through* him:

> *When we encounter someone whom the world regards as trash, we so-to-say lay Christ's image over that one, so that Christ imaginatively catalyses a change in the way we value that person.*
> DON CUPITT

And in valuing others through Christ, as Christ values them, seeing them indeed 'as Christ' ('whatever you do to one of these, however lowly, you do to me,' he told his followers), we ourselves become Christlike. To save others is to be saved. To value others

is to become of value ourselves. Once we can discern Christ in
the stranger, the rest becomes easy. Well, relatively easy.

The Fat Lady

J. D. Salinger concludes his novel *Franny and Zooey* with a
powerful scene.

Franny and Zooey are sister and brother who had been child
stars on the radio together. Franny is depressed about her acting
career. Zooey rings her long-distance and tells her of an event
from their shared past on the show 'It's a Wise Child', with their
brother Seymour.

> *'Anyway, I started bitching one night before the broadcast.
> Seymour'd told me to shine my shoes just as I was going out
> the door... I was furious. The studio audience were all
> morons, the announcer was a moron, the sponsors were
> morons, and I just damn well wasn't going to shine my
> shoes for them, I told Seymour.'*

Seymour had told him to shine them anyway: to shine them
'for the Fat Lady'.

> *'He never did tell me who the Fat Lady was, but I shined my
> shoes for the Fat Lady every time I ever went on the air
> again.'*

For years he had done this without missing the ritual more
than a couple of times. And he always had before his eyes a clear
picture of that Fat Lady.

> *'I had her sitting on this porch all day, swatting flies, with
> her radio going full-blast from morning till night. I figured
> the heat was terrible, and she probably had cancer, and—*

I don't know. Anyway, it seemed goddam clear why Seymour wanted me to shine my shoes when I went on the air. It made sense.'

Franny was now standing, holding the phone with both hands. 'He told me, too,' she said, 'He told me to be funny for the Fat Lady, once...'

And she too had pictured the Fat Lady with cancer, listening all day long to the radio. Zooey, sensing his moment, interrupts:

'I don't care where an actor acts. It can be in summer stock, it can be over a radio, it can be over television, it can be in a goddam Broadway theatre, complete with the most fashionable, most well-fed, most sunburned-looking audience you can imagine. But I'll tell you a terrible secret—Are you listening to me? There isn't anyone out there who isn't Seymour's Fat Lady... There isn't anyone anywhere that isn't Seymour's Fat Lady. Don't you know that?... And don't you know... who that Fat Lady really is?... It's Christ Himself. Christ Himself, buddy.'

For joy, apparently, it was all that Franny could do to hold the phone, even with both hands.

J. D. SALINGER

45 Sex and Education...

The Lover?

Everyone is at it these days. According to the stickers in the back windows of cars, all sorts of trades, professions and vocations do it in all sorts of unlikely positions. You can tune in to it on TV, though only after 9p.m.—when Granny (the only one of the family today still to be embarrassed) has nodded off.

And then there are the books...

Is that the Student Bookshop?

> *Yes, how can I help you?*

Er, well... I... Do you stock sex books?

> *Oh yes, sir, we have a wide selection:* The Joy of Sex, More Joy of Sex, The Joy of More Sex, The Vegetarian Cookbook and Sex Manual, Sex for Train Spotters...

Great, great. Look, I have to have some rather explicit, technical publications from the Dirtymac Press: The Mechanics and Hydraulics of the Orgasm *and* Degree Level Revision Notes on Bonking.

> *I see. They will be for the coarse course, of course?*

Pardon?

> *At the polytechnic, sorry... university. Dr Pervert's course on 'The Deconstruction of Sexual Bonding in Post-modern Culture, with particular reference to Jacques Derrida, Jürgen Habermas and Madonna'.*

Yes, that's it.

> *No problem, we have plenty of copies of both.*

*Great. Er, but do I have to, like... **ask** for them? Will they be, like, under the counter?*

Of course not, sir, our policy is to put all such material on open shelves. There's nothing to be ashamed about in sex, you know. We aren't in the Victorian era now.

Well, no... of course not...

Will there be anything else?

Oh yes. I'd like a copy of the Bible.

The Bible. Well, you'll have to ask. We do keep **them** *under the counter, naturally. Special requests only. So as not to give offence to others, you know.*

Oh, quite. It was just that I heard this bit from the Song of Songs on TV. It sounded a bit, you know, randy. I thought I could use it in my dissertation.

Oh, why didn't you say so, sir? We have a separate, explicitly illustrated, edition of the Song of Songs in stock. I'm pretty sure that it's shelved next to Yoghurt Makers Do It with Culture.

Fine, I'll be in Wednesday. Do you take credit cards? Swedish Sexpress?

That will do nicely.

Getting it right

You can get Do-it-Yourself and How-it-Works manuals for everything nowadays. And sex is no exception. Like the young cook and the beginner gardener, anyone who can read—or at least look at pictures—can now perform successfully. Videos are available for those who prefer less static sex education, or are put off by books with long words.

But *technique* is not everything, either. It takes two to get it right, and getting it right is more than, and at times can often ignore, getting the anatomy and physiology right. Sexual relationships after all are *relationships*. And relationships between people engage all of each of them. Passion engages the 'passions': the feelings that lie at the very core of human personality. Sex combines hearts, minds and souls, as well as bodies.

Christianity says that sex is OK. Perhaps it doesn't say this loudly enough. Despite its reputation as a prudish religion, the sacred scriptures of Christianity proclaim that sex is God's inven-tion. And the Song of Songs *does* celebrate physical sex: it rejoices in human randiness. It's more than just OK, then. Sex is a divine gift, a part of the creation, and therefore, at the very least, 'very good'.

Sex is essentially about creation. 'Procreation' is the sharing of creative love so as to love another human being into existence. But its creative power is wider even than this. It can create a bond between two people that is not only deeply fulfilling and satisfying, but also cannot be left under the duvet.

Traditional Christian injunctions about 'no sex outside marriage' at least acknowledge this: that this powerhouse of creative emotions and relationships is too potent to be given unlimited freedom. 'Sexual licence', 'putting it about', 'sowing your wild oats' sound as if they are celebrations of freedom. But true freedom, *grown-up* freedom, acknowledges the responsibility that freedom brings. And being grown-up about sex involves a recognition that this (often sexist) licence can be a licence to kill. It can do this literally through AIDS, or psychologically where trust and love is destroyed by another's sexual unfaithfulness. It can do it—in an odd inversion—by the birth of unwanted children.

Sex is always more than sex. It can be life. It can be death.

Religious randiness

The Bible has no illusions about the power of sex. The sneer that religion is against sex has in fact little support from Scripture, even ignoring the Song of Songs. In the Old Testament, it would appear, they are all at it: begetting right, left and centre. Some of it reads as if it has come straight off the tabloid press: mixing sex, monarchy and religion in equal parts. In the Second Book of Samuel, for example, the Prophet Nathan had to have a stern word with King David on the subject of coveting his neighbour's wife to excess; the excess being that he seduced Bathsheba when her husband Uriah was away in the army, got her pregnant and then ensured that Uriah didn't come home from the next battle.

227

Time and again the prophets railed against the nation because Israel, God's people, was sleeping around, religiously speaking. It is not that all sex—and only sex—was seen as sin in the Old Testament. It is rather that sin, especially the ultimate Israelite sin of turning their backs on their God and worshipping idols, was described as illicit sex. Israel was described as acting like a prostitute, sleeping with everyone but God, her husband. You can't get away from sex in the Old Testament.

And what about the New? According to Paul's letter to the Ephesians, the Christian church is 'the bride of Christ'. She is expected to be faithful to her husband, to be close to him, bonded to him, made fruitful by him. Rejection, even divorce, are possible, of course. And adultery is always a temptation. The risks of sex are always there. But she is expected to be faithful, as Jesus is faithful to her.

The image shows that the church cannot be simply 'against sex', for the highest language ascribed to the church is that of a sexual partner. Sex is that natural. Properly used, directed and harnessed it is *the* metaphor for true religion.

> There is no better image of the Church.... It... must be penetrated by the spirit of God to its most secret depths. And when so penetrated, it is united to him in one flesh, one organism, its whole being invaded by his love, pregnant and fertile with his ripening purposes.
>
> Anthony Bridge

> Sex is bad for one. (But it's great for two.)
>
> T-shirt

A kind of loving

But love, of course, is more than sex. And the love of God for his creatures and even for his church is broader and more unqualified than the language of sex suggests. Scholars have at times distinguished between erotic or need-love, which is evoked by the attractiveness of its object, and God's unconditional *agape* or gift-love. This is a love that extends even to the unlovely— God's unconditional, universal love for all. When Christians speak of love, even in the context of sexual love, they have always to remind themselves that true love must contain something of this *agape*, and therefore must be more than a matter of seeking self-satisfaction.

This is active love directed towards the good of the other person. In the end, it may go beyond self completely, beyond attraction completely, and beyond feelings completely. It is the supreme love; the love that God alone can purely give but that we can at least begin to attempt. It is the love about which Paul wrote in his first letter to the Corinthians (who knew all about sex): the love that transcends selfishness, and whose endurance is without limit. This love, Paul says, 'will last for ever'. An earlier translation, and earlier writers, called it 'charity'.

It is truly a transformation of human love. It is the mark of the grace of God.

My father told me all about the birds and the bees. The liar. I went steady with a woodpecker till I was twenty-one.

Bob Hope

I heard an old religious man
But yesternight declare
That he had found a text to prove
That only God, my dear,
Can love you for yourself alone
And not your yellow hair.

W. B. Yeats

46 Inclusive Conclusion...

The Multinational Corporation?

In the mid 1960s a primary-school teacher in small-town America undertook a daring experiment to illustrate to her class the meaning of racial prejudice.

She introduced it as a game and told the children that, for a day, blue eyes were bad and brown eyes were good. They entered into her game with gusto.

But their pleasure in it turned to fear for some, as the blue-eyed children were made to sit at the back of the class. They took second turns for everything and had their every utterance ridiculed. 'That's just the sort of stupid thing a blue-eyes would say,' the teacher scolded, and she gave them the blame for any misdemeanour that occurred.

But worst of all were the collars. So that they could be recognized from a distance, the blue-eyed children were forced to wear collars. It soon became the collar and not the blue eyes that served as the focus of prejudice and discrimination. The collar split up friendships. Brown-eyed children were very quick to turn against their blue-eyed class mates and identify with their own 'superior' group.

The following day the teacher turned the tables. Now blue eyes were good and brown eyes were bad. The blue-eyed children did not need to be told twice to take off their collars and put them on their brown-eyed 'friends'.

The effect of that collar was frightening in many ways. It even affected the way the children who wore it performed academically. They scored several points lower than on their non-collar days. One little boy particularly showed symptoms of trauma, becoming at first withdrawn and then aggressive.

On the third day the teacher spent a long time discussing the experiment: 'How did you feel?' 'Why did you do that?' 'How do you think other people felt?' Years later, the group met again as adults and watched their reactions on a film taken at the time. All agreed that it had given them a deep insight that they could not have gained without the experiment.

Being different

In north Northumberland there is a herd of wild cattle, the only one in existence in Britain. The white cattle of Chillingham cannot be approached too closely, for the bulls will attempt to kill any intruder. They are a pure inbreeding herd; and so far they have resisted all that nature's storms and diseases have thrown at them.

But it is a hard society. Weak, old or sick cattle are set upon by the herd and gored to death. If a new calf shows any blemish—any divergence from the white-coat-with-red-ears norm—it is killed by the herd, or left to die of starvation. Racism is thus built into the breed. They display a sort of original ethnic cleansing.

This is all natural enough, biologically. The whole herd may be put at risk by slow or diseased members. Even their 'racial purity' behaviour is understandable. Individuals of one species must mate with their own kind, or a species will die out. We can only breed with those who look like us. And in an inbreeding community a difference in looks may mark an enfeebling mutation. This seems to have been taken to extremes by the Chillingham cattle, but they have their excuses.

Human racists do not. What begins as a proper sense of solidarity-with-those-who-are-like-us, and therefore of separation from the rest, is easily perverted into Paki-bashing, queer-baiting and real ethnic cleansing in Bosnia and Rwanda.

Natural separations of a fairly broad kind have often been sharpened by society and ignorance into prejudice and discrimination against anyone who looks a little different, or talks funny (with the wrong accent, or in the wrong language).

Biologically this is absurd, for all human beings—black, white, red, brown, yellow—are one species. But we are sometimes very good at absurdity.

Breaking barriers

The Old Testament was not immune from this sort of moral corruption. Purity of race was mixed with a concern for purity of religion in many passages in the Law: passages that specify who can and who cannot 'enter the congregation of the Lord'. And by the time of Jesus the list of those who had to be kept out was very long: Gentiles, lepers, the mixed-race Samaritans, women, tax-collectors...

But show Jesus a category, and he breaks it. He overturned the purity laws; declared all food clean; touched corpses and lepers; talked with women and sat at the same table with prostitutes and tax-collectors—the social and religious outcasts of their day.

His church too claims to be 'catholic', that is to say *universal*, embracing the whole world. Paul tells the first Christians that they are 'neither Jew nor Greek, slave nor free, male nor female; for you are all one in Christ Jesus'. The church is called to be all-embracing by a Lord who is colour-blind and does not stop to ask your sex, ethnic background, class, bank balance, country of origin, or taste in music or alcohol, before (or even after) he calls you to follow him.

Of course the church louses up the plan sometimes. In fact, to be frank, it does so very often. There have been, and still are, churches that are in favour of racial apartheid, churches that are intended only for the middle classes, and churches that up-front or deep-down reject women.

But whenever the church sees the true breadth of its calling, it has become ashamed of such a narrow-hearted Christianity. For on the cross, Christians have said, Jesus' arms embrace the whole world.

United—or fallen

It is difficult to be a Christian on your own. Perhaps it is impossible. To be a disciple of Jesus is to be called (as an individual) to follow him. But on the road behind Jesus the new convert finds many other fellow disciples. To follow Jesus is to become part of that community of the road.

Biblical religion is never purely personal and individual. Sin and salvation are both social concepts. My wrongdoing affects you, but so does my love for you. So Archbishop Michael Ramsey could write: '"Individualism"... has no place in Christianity', adding that it is through the death of individualism that the individual truly finds herself or himself.

The church is also, as a hymn puts it, 'all one body'. Despite the splits and schisms, divisions and denominations, it shows a sort of unity. Many Christians recognize these divisions as a disgrace, or at least as unimportant reflections of a proper variety in being Christian. Others wish to perpetuate them, claiming that there is only one, true church which—not surprisingly—is the one of which they are proud to be a member.

All such debates pile metaphor upon metaphor. We speak glibly of 'bodies' and 'members', forgetting that this language is only really at home in the medical textbooks ('corporate' and 'corporation' are derived from the Latin word for a body, *corpus*). Paul is mainly responsible for the metaphor of the church as a body. But for him it wasn't so much *a* body as *the* Body: the Body *of Christ*. 'Christ is like a single body with its many limbs and organs, which, many as they are, together make up one body.' Therefore Christians are said to 'belong to one another', for 'if one organ suffers, they all suffer together. If one flourishes, they all rejoice together'.

As with much Christian doctrine about the church, however, this is a truth that people are called towards, rather than a reality they already show. 'Is Christ divided?' asks Paul, expecting the answer, 'Of course not!' But the church of the first century clearly was divided. And so is its twentieth-century successor: not just across denominations but within congregations. The church is *not* one, and it does not behave like a body of interdependent members.

Yet that is what God calls it to be. That is what, as religious people claim, God *intends* for it. And God's intention, his hope for the church, is the more significant thing. In a sense it is more 'real' than the squabbling, sulking, sinful, outpatients' clinic that we call 'the church militant here on earth'.

So the church must make itself real, become what it is called to be, become its true self. As the Anglican theologians Anthony and Richard Hanson put it:

> *This does not mean that the church is a kind of unattainable ideal, a castle in the air, a star to which we can hitch our wagon, any more than it means that Christ is out of our reach, imprisoned in some inaccessible perfection.*
>
> A. T. & R. P. C. HANSON

Such a view is contradicted by the idea of the incarnation: God becoming human in Christ (see Chapter 38). Rather, 'the church is *there*, given. But we must realize it.'

So this is the corporate purpose of the disciples of Jesus, to 'realize' the church—to make it into a reality. *Individually* they are to follow his way, to find Christ in one another and to be Christ to one another. *Together* they are to be his body, passing on his good news and his healing love in service to all.

That's what it's all about.

That is corporate Christianity.

Acknowledgments

We would like to thank all those who have given us permission to include extracts in this book. If there are any inadvertent omissions or inaccuracies in these acknowledgments we apologize to those concerned. Each figure refers to the page number of an extract.

P14   From *The Meaning of Liff* by Douglas Adams and John Lloyd, Faber & Faber
       From 'Personality' by Carl Sandburg in *The Wheel*, edited by Emiline Garnett, Burns & Oates/Macmillan, London, 1965, reprinted by permission of Burns & Oates

P19   From 'Meditation' by Ezra Pound in *The Wheel*, edited by Emiline Garnett, Burns & Oates/Macmillan, London, 1965, reprinted by permission of Burns & Oates

P23   From the Revised English Bible © 1989 by permission of Oxford and Cambridge University Presses

P24   From 'Aurora Leigh' by Elizabeth Barrett Browning

P26   From *Pensées*, Blaise Pascal

P40   From a letter to *The Independent* from Richard Dawkins, Saturday 20 March 1993

P45   Quoted in *Priestland's Progress*, Gerald Priestland

P54   From *In Search of Christianity*, edited by Tony Moss, Firethorn/Water-stone, London, 1986

P58   From 'Heaven' by Rupert Brooke

P67   From 'The Font' by Clive Sansom in *The Wheel*, edited by Emiline Garnett, Burns & Oates/Macmillan, London, 1965, reprinted by permission of Burns & Oates

P69   Czech carol
       From 'Mid-Winter' by Christina Rossetti

P73   From 'The Death of the Hired Man' in *Robert Frost: Selected Poems*, Penguin, Harmondsworth, 1973, reprinted by permission of Jonathan Cape/Random House

P74   From the Revised English Bible © 1989 by permission of Oxford and Cambridge University Presses

P75   From *The Shaking of the Foundations*, Paul Tillich, Pelican, Harmondsworth, 1962

P88   From 'Do not go gentle into that good night' by Dylan Thomas, *Collected Poems*, Dent: London, 1939, by permission of David Higham Associates

P88-89 From *God and the Universe of Faiths*, John Hick, Macmillan, Basingstoke, 1973

P94   From *selected poems 1923-1958*, e.e. cummings, Faber & Faber, London, 1960, reprinted by permission of W.W. Norton Co. Inc., New York

P102   From the Revised English Bible © 1989 by permission of Oxford and Cambridge University Presses

P108   From *A Rumour of Angels*, Peter L. Berger, Penguin, Harmondsworth, 1970

P110   From the Revised Standard Version of the Bible © 1946. 1952. 1971 by the
        Division of Christian Education of the National Council of Churches of Christ
        in the USA and used by permission

P113   From 'Time does not heal' by Elizabeth Jennings, reprinted by permission of
        David Higham Associates

P121   From *Son of Man*, Dennis Potter, Penguin, Harmondsworth, reprinted by
        permission of Judy Dace Associates

P125   From *Markings*, Dag Hammarskjöld, Faber & Faber, London, 1964

P127   From the Jerusalem Bible, © 1966, 1967, 1968 by Darton, Longman and
        Todd Ltd and Doubleday and Company, Inc. All rights reserved.

P131   From the Revised English Bible © 1989 by permission of Oxford and
        Cambridge University Presses

P132   From *Evil and the God of Love*, John Hick, Collins/Fontana, Glasgow, 1968

P150   From *Life Maps* by Jim Fowler and Sam Keen, edited by Jerome Berryman,
        Winston Press, Waco, Texas, 1978

P169   From *Room at the Top* by John Braine, Mandarin, London, 1991

P174   From 'That Nature is a Heraclitean Fire and the Comfort of the Resurrection',
        Poems and Prose of Gerard Manley Hopkins, Penguin, Harmondsworth, 1953

P184   From *Centuries of Meditations*, Thomas Traherne
        From the Revised English Bible © 1989 by permission of Oxford and
        Cambridge University Presses

P207   From *Struggle and Fulfilment*, Donald Evans, Collins, Cleveland, 1979

P210   From 'Eleanor Rigby' by Lennon/McCartney
        From 'September 1, 1939', *W.H. Auden: Selected Poems*, Faber & Faber,
        London, 1979

P222   From *The New Christian Ethics*, Don Cupitt, SCM, London, 1988

P223   From the Revised English Bible © 1989 by permission of Oxford and
        Cambridge University Presses

P223-24 From *Franny and Zooey*, J.D. Salinger, Penguin, Harmondsworth, 1964

P228   From 'God and the Church' by Anthony Bridge in *Sermons from Great St
        Mary's*, edited by Hugh Montefiore

P229   From 'For Anne Gregory', W.B. Yeats

P234   From *The Identity of the Church*, A.T. and R.P.C. Hanson

Index of Themes